EVERYTHING

YOU NEED TO KNOW ABOUT...

Dog Training

GERILYN J. BIELAKIEWICZ

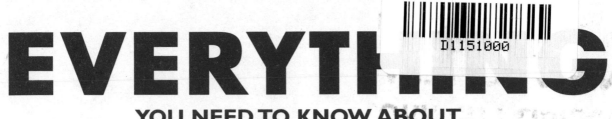

David & Charles

A DAVID & CHARLES BOOK
David & Charles is a subsidiary of F+W (UK) Ltd.,
an F+W Publications Inc. company

First published in the UK in 2004
Reprinted in 2007
First published in the USA as The Everything® Dog Training and Tricks Book,
by Adams Media Corporation in 2003

Project Manager Ian Kearey
Cover Design Ali Myer

A catalogue record for this book is available from the British Library.

10 Digit ISBN 0 7153 2062 9
13 Digit ISBN 9780715320624

Printed in Great Britain by CPI Bath
for David & Charles
Brunel House   Newton Abbot   Devon

Visit our website at www.davidandcharles.co.uk

David & Charles books are available from all good bookshops;
alternatively you can contact our Orderline on (0)1626 334555 or
write to us at FREEPOST EX2110, David & Charles Direct,
Newton Abbot, TQ12 4ZZ (no stamp required UK mainland).

Dedication

I dedicate this book to my husband, Paul,
whose love, support and encouragement
have helped me achieve my dreams.

Acknowledgments

Thank you, Mum, for looking after my sons
while I wrote, making it possible for this book
to become a reality.

Contents

Introduction

Training your dog is a way to bring about a line of communication, a common language that you will use to communicate with your dog for his entire lifetime. Whether you spend time teaching your dog simple obedience commands or complicated tricks, you will expand your relationship with your dog and build a strong foundation of trust. Developing a trusting relationship with your dog through the use of positive training methods will not only enhance the special bond that you share with your dog, but it will also make the quality of life you share all the better. I can't think of a more exciting adventure than to train a dog and learn how his mind works and how he communicates. I think that, with practice, you will find that dogs are wonderfully intelligent and have a great sense of humour. Having worked with dogs for more than half of my life, and having taught close to 2,000 people how to train their dogs, I can honestly say that training a dog is a journey you don't want to miss.

Training is a relationship, and, as with all relationships, it needs to be maintained through lots of repetition and practice. There is no designated beginning or end to training, since a dog is capable of learning throughout its entire lifetime. Initially, training involves lots of practice and will probably include attending classes to learn how to practise when surrounded by distractions. Eventually, even though you may not train your dog formally every day, your dog will still be learning new things every day – and participating in that learning experience is what owning a dog is all about.

Behaviour problems can be detrimental to establishing a relationship with your dog and keeping it strong, and I have addressed several of the most trying ones in this book. The solutions are simple and concentrate on rebuilding trust in your relationship with your dog, while at the same time improving your dog's manners and comfort. Almost every behaviour problem relates back to some need that has not been met. You will notice a pattern as you read about the solutions to each problem: a lot of dogs would not exhibit behaviour problems if they got enough exercise. If your dog is experiencing a behaviour problem that is threatening your sanity, consider increasing his daily exercise and see if this doesn't help alleviate some of the intensity of the problem.

The topics covered in this book range from teaching tricks to solving behaviour problems, and I hope it in some way inspires you to build a great relationship with your dog and have fun doing it. There is no greater reward for your hard effort than the loyalty and love of a faithful canine companion. Great dog companions – like great human companions – are cultivated, not born, by spending time together, learning about each other and learning how to develop the strongest relationship that you can. It is my sincere wish that this book will positively change the way you view dog training and enhance your relationship with your dog.

Why Teach Tricks?

Teaching tricks is a must for every dog owner who thinks of their pet as part of the family. Training a dog is like any other relationship; it is partly about establishing rules and boundaries (what is and isn't acceptable), partly about teaching your dog what is expected of him, and partly about enjoying each other's company.

Training Improves Your Relationship

From the moment you bring your new puppy into your home, he is learning how to get along with your family, a species entirely different from his own. If your instructions are vague and inconsistent, his confusion about what is acceptable will manifest itself in undesirable behaviour and mischief. If you spend time teaching him what is expected of him, you will be rewarded with a well-mannered pet that becomes a beloved member of your family. As I often tell my students, you get what you reinforce. If you pay attention to what your dog is doing, you'll reap the rewards of a well-behaved dog.

Boston Terrier
with duck
friend

Teaching tricks is about having fun and being a little silly, but it can also greatly benefit a frustrated owner and an overactive dog. Teaching your dog to roll over, play dead or sit may seem a bit frivolous until you realize that in order to do those tricks your dog must have some basic understanding of the Sit or Lie Down commands. Teaching tricks capitalizes and improves upon what the dog already knows and makes it better. A goofy energetic dog will not jump up at visitors, for instance, if you can teach him a show-stopping Play Dead trick to perform. Another benefit of trick training is that it improves public relations – doggie PR – with non-dog-lovers.

Dogs that can perform tricks are perceived as friendly to most non-dog people, which can improve their idea of your dog. What nervous person could resist a dog that says his prayers, rolls over and plays dead?

The beauty of teaching tricks is that they can be taught to any dog of any size, breed or temperament; you are limited only by the dog's physical ability to perform the task. I think it's crucial for larger dogs, especially those whose breed alone makes people nervous, to learn some fun and silly tricks that they can do when they meet new people. People will react totally differently to a big silly German Shepherd balancing a biscuit on his nose than they would to one sitting politely. This also has an added benefit for your dog: the more relaxed visitors are, the more your dog will like having them around.

Trick Training Leads to Better Training

Teaching tricks can help you control a dog that barks too much or shakes and shivers when he meets new people, simply by giving him a more acceptable alternative. Trick training will make you a better dog trainer, a person who knows how to motivate their dog and has learned how to break things down into small parts. Since training your dog is a lifelong process, the more you practise the skills of a good dog trainer, the better you will get at it – and the more quickly your dog will learn.

The most difficult part of being a beginner is that you are learning at the same time as you are trying to teach your dog. Be patient with yourself – dog training is a physical skill that requires lots of practice and repetition. You will reap the rewards a hundredfold the first time it all comes together and your dog performs perfectly.

Performing tricks keeps old dogs young, agile and flexible, and gives young, energetic dogs an outlet for their energy.

To teach tricks, you will find you need to be able to break things down into component steps that are easily achieved in a training session. You will get really good at knowing how much information your dog will need in order to succeed at a given trick, and exactly when to withdraw the extra help so that your dog can perform on his own. These skills come with time and practice, but there are several things you can do to help speed up the process.

1. Keep a notebook to record your training sessions.
2. Before you begin, map out the steps involved in teaching the trick.
3. Make sure you make your plan flexible, and be ready to add more detailed steps if your dog has trouble understanding what you want.
4. Arm yourself with the best treats and rewards to keep your dog interested and motivated.
5. Time your sessions; try not to make them longer than five minutes.
6. Read through the chapter on clicker training and be sure to familiarize yourself with how it works; it will save you a lot of time in the long run.
7. Try to stick to the plan you've mapped out; don't click the dog for lots of different tricks in one session.
8. If you get stuck on one particular trick, discuss with a friend about how to help your dog through it.
9. Add in distractions as soon as the dog starts to get the hang of what you're trying to teach.
10. Don't be afraid to go backwards and review previous steps if your dog's behaviour falls apart in a new place.

In general, being a good trainer is best indicated by your dog's attitude. If you keep sessions upbeat and fun, make it easy for your dog to succeed and always make sure that you end the training session on a positive note, it won't be long before your dog thinks that working with you is better than anything else in the world.

The Importance of Consistency

Practising on a regular basis is important if you want to become a good trainer and you want to accomplish the goals you've established for your dog. Designating a time to practise several times a week ensures that you will have lots of opportunities to experiment with techniques, and your dog will have lots of time to get the hang of working with you.

If you have a problem, or a new trick, success will come more easily if you block out specific times during the week and give yourself permission to drop everything for your dog. As you get better at including training in your weekly routine (or daily routine if your dog is young and learning the basics of living politely with humans), you will realize how easy the whole process is. You'll also appreciate how much fun it is to have a dog that works with you because he enjoys it.

Go to Class

Some people find it difficult to block out time for training; they need the consistency of being enrolled in a group class to motivate themselves to practise. Many training groups offer more than obedience classes; some offer ringcraft, agility classes, tricks classes, fly ball, tracking, hunting, herding or other types of dog sports. Learning something new is more fun when you have the right tools and support – so make sure that the training group's philosophy matches your own and that you feel comfortable there.

tips

As you search for the right dog-training class, remember that dog training doesn't require the use of force. If you are having problems with your dog's behaviour, he needs more training, not heavy-handed corrections and reprimands.

Strengthen Your Relationship With Your Dog

When you are training your dog, you are teaching him to share a common language. Teaching your dog the meaning of the basic obedience commands gives you a vocabulary with which to communicate in day-to-day interactions with your dog. As with any communication, you and your dog need to understand each other. Once you find a way that works for you, don't change it. Otherwise, you are likely to confuse your dog and frustrate yourself.

Most people who train their dogs past the basics really begin to appreciate communicating with another species. Specialized training expands your bond with your dog and lets you communicate on a higher level. You will be amazed at just how intelligent dogs are, and at what can be accomplished through training.

The strong bonds developed through training carry over in play and in all the fun things you do with your dog. If your dog likes to swim in the sea and you like to walk on the beach, think of how much more enjoyable your time together will be if, when the walk is over, you can simply summon your dog and leave.

Stop Behaviour Problems

Teaching tricks can help you be more creative about solving behaviour problems with your dog. If you take the time to evaluate why your dog is doing what he is doing, you will figure out a solution that works for you. Some dogs that bark too much are quieter if they are allowed to carry a toy to the visitor. Dogs that jump can learn to do a Bow or Sit and Wave in exchange for petting from guests, or do their best version of Roll Over or Play Dead if you need to relax a non-dog-person who is afraid of your dog.

Whatever the problem, use tricks in place of the inappropriate behaviour to redirect the dog's energy and enthusiasm. The key here is to make sure that you practise the trick in all different kinds of environments with all different kinds of distractions until your dog's response to the cue is immediate and perfect. The more distraction-proof your tricks are, the more useful they will be to you when you ask your dog to do them.

Exercise for the Energetic Dog

You will find that dogs with lots of energy are really good at learning tricks. They offer a lot of natural traits that are easy to capitalize upon and turn into a trick. Little dogs love to stand on their hind legs or jump in place to see what's on the table, for instance, while big dogs like to spin in circles or stand on their hind legs to take a look out of the window or to get your attention.

Self-Control

Training energetic dogs is fun because they don't tire as easily as other dogs, and they are always willing to try something new. An energetic dog will go along with just about any trick you can dream up; they live for attention any way they can get it. Combining a stroll in the park with tricks can both give your dog a satisfying workout and at the same time teach him manners and self-control.

Teaching your dog simple tricks in one- to three-minute sessions several times a day can help alleviate boredom and create a more contented dog. Giving your dog something to think about is a definite furniture-saver, but it does not replace common sense about using gates, crates and pens to keep your dog from getting into trouble in your absence.

Most people who own energetic dogs complain at some point about the dog's lack of self-control. Dogs don't just grow out of this; without training, they will not one day wake up and be better behaved. If you don't put the time into training your dog to have better overall manners, you will live with a whirling dervish that never learns to socialize with people.

Know the Limits

Performing tricks requires some measure of control on the dog's part because he has to pay attention to your cues and get feedback on what's going right. Dogs that are constantly on the move need skilled trainers who can give them lots of feedback and break the exercise down into tiny steps. Trying to push such dogs too far too fast will result in frustration for both of you. Teaching a dog should be fun, regardless of what you train your dog to do. The end result will be a dog that is an enjoyable companion and a treasured member of your family.

Therapy Work

If you need some good reasons to teach your dog lots of tricks, think about the benefits of visiting nursing homes and hospitals. Share your dog's talents with patients who may have owned a dog at some point, but who, due to their health circumstances, can no longer have a dog as a part of their lives. These people might really appreciate the warm, loving companionship of a well-behaved dog.

If you and your dog are visiting patients one to one or in a group, use tricks to break the ice and to get people to warm towards your dog. Tricks are a great opening for conversations with patients, and you'll often see everyone visibly relax and smile when they see your dog do anything remotely silly. I've found in all my years of visiting that dogs don't have to do much to make people happy.

Large and dark dogs can sometimes be scary to non-dog-people or children. What better way to introduce your dog to someone than to have him do a trick that makes your visitors smile and relax? Play Dead and Roll Over are great for relaxing a non-dog-owning guest.

Trick training is something anyone can do, and getting out there and showing people how much fun it is can be a great way to educate the public about the importance of establishing a relationship with their dog. Whatever the reason to teach tricks, the bottom line is to have fun. It is my aim in writing this book to get you hooked on training your dog! So why not find some tricks in the successive chapters and see how much fun you can have teaching your dog something new.

Chapter 2

What's Your Dog Like?

Taking a moment to get an idea of 'who' your dog is can help you design a training programme that will be effective in teaching him to fit in with your family. Finding out how your dog responds to distractions and whether he's motivated by toys or games may be helpful in putting together a programme that is easy to implement.

How Well Do You Know Your Dog?

Breaking your training sessions down into small steps, finding out what motivates your dog, and finding out where your dog is most distracted, will help you know where to start. Below are some questions you might want to ask yourself before you begin your training programme.

·   Is he energetic or laid-back? A maniac retriever or a lazy spaniel?
·   Does he do something that you've always meant to curb but didn't know how to?
·   Is his attention span short or long? How does he respond when there are distractions?
·   What is his favourite treat or toy?
·   Does he give up easily, or does he persist until he gets the job done?

Understanding your dog's personality and learning style is essential to teaching him tricks – or anything else – enjoyably and successfully. Combining an energetic dog with a fast-moving and smart trick is exciting and invigorating not only for the dog, but also for your audience. Knowing your dog includes knowing what motivates him. Finding just the right kind of treat, toy or game will help your dog associate training with fun and help your training programme be a success on all levels.

Energy Level

Some dogs are laid-back; others run circles around us all day. Differences in breed, temperament and personality all come into play when designing a successful training programme. Living with your dog makes you the expert when it comes to knowing the ins and outs of his personality and just what will work for him. Paying attention to how active your dog is can help you learn about his personality and help you choose a trick that will be easy and fun to teach.

Highly Active

Active dogs love active tricks because they make the most of natural behaviour, such as spinning, jumping, barking and pawing. When dogs have this much energy, take advantage of their abilities and teach appropriate tricks.

If you are new to training and are having a hard time keeping up with your dog, don't be afraid to hire a professional trainer to coach you. The more skills you gain as your dog's trainer, the better you will be able to help your dog understand what you are trying to teach him.

However, high-energy dogs get overstimulated easily, and do best in short, concise training sessions with clear goals in mind. If you don't push a high-energy dog to work for long periods, he will fall in love with learning tricks.

Less Active

Lower-energy dogs may be harder to get moving until they have worked out what you want them to do. These dogs are thinkers, and they like to know where you're going with all this. Go slowly with your dog. Try to keep your sessions short, because such dogs often bore easily and hate repeating things too many times in a row. Training before a meal (using favourite treats as rewards) often perks them up and lets you get in a good training session.

Medium-energy dogs are the easiest to work with because they allow you to make a lot of mistakes and be less organized. They don't mind repeating things over and over, and they are patient with you when you make mistakes or haven't planned out what you are trying to teach. Dogs with moderate energy levels are laid-back and fun, turning their energy on like a rocket booster when they need to, but generally going along with whatever you're doing.

Personality

Ask yourself some questions about your dog's personality traits to discover where to begin your training programme. It can save a lot of time if you start training your dog in an environment that isn't so distracting that he can't pay attention. An outgoing dog will love tricks that he can perform in a crowd, while a quieter dog may prefer performing at a bit of a distance. Teaching your dog where he is most relaxed and least distracted or worried will help him be successful.

Social Temperament

A dog that is easily distracted by his friendliness around people will benefit from training sessions that start somewhere quiet, then quickly move on to involve the distractions he finds hard to resist. Training your dog to perform tricks around distractions from the start is one way to ensure that his performance will not fall apart in public.

Shy dogs, on the other hand, may resist doing tricks in public until they are more confident. With this type of dog, practise in the most comfortable environment possible and then gradually integrate distractions with familiar people. The ultimate goal is to incorporate strangers and new places so that your dog can perform anywhere.

How do you work with your dog around distractions?
If you can't get your dog's attention in 10–15 seconds, start by putting some distance between your dog and the distraction. Increasing the distance will make it easier for your dog to focus and perform the exercise. As he gains confidence and learns to pay attention, you can then decrease the distance slowly without his being distracted.

Special Talents and Interests

Depending on a dog's breed characteristics, he will often display a natural talent for certain tricks. For instance, Labradors and Golden Retrievers often excel at tricks that involve having things in their mouths, such as

Put Away Your Toys or Fetch Me a Drink from the Fridge. Herding breeds might prefer to learn directional tricks like spinning to the left or right. A small dog that stands on its hind legs a lot may be a great candidate to learn Sit Up and Beg or Dance. A large-breed dog may be perfect for Play Dead, especially if he is of the low-energy type.

The most important thing to remember here is that any dog can master tricks that are physically possible for it to do. Dogs are amazing creatures, and they are so willing to be with us and please us that they will put up with a lot so long as they are getting some attention. With enough patience and practice, and the right training tools, you can teach your dog to do just about anything!

Keep Safety in Mind

Keep your dog's safety in mind while you are training, and pay attention to its physical limitations. If you have a long-backed breed, a Basset Hound for instance, it may not be a good idea to teach him to Sit Up Pretty, since his torso would be extremely heavy to support on such short legs. For larger breeds, such as Great Danes and Saint Bernards, you may not want to do any tricks that involve jumping, since the impact of landing is not good for their joints.

If your dog refuses to assume a certain position, don't be afraid to have him checked for an injury. Dogs are stoical animals and rarely show discomfort unless it's obvious. Hiding injuries is instinctive, stemming from their wolf cousins, who live by the rule of survival of the fittest.

Pay attention to your dog's weight as well, since extra kilos can lead to injuries. If you respect your dog's physical limitations, he will amaze you with his willingness to try what you ask. A dog cannot tell you if something is uncomfortable, so do your best to read his body language and go slowly. As often as possible, perform on a soft surface like a rug, grass or sand, especially for tricks involving jumping, spinning or rolling.

Being aware of your environment will minimize injuries and make your dog more comfortable.

What Motivates Your Dog?

Learning what your dog likes as rewards is crucial to being a successful dog trainer. Many people are surprised to learn that dog biscuits and dry dog food just don't work. Be creative in what you offer your dog as rewards, and keep the pieces tiny if it's food. Even a Great Dane shouldn't get a treat larger than 6mm (1/4in). Keeping the treats tiny will ensure that you'll be able to train for a longer period of time, because your dog won't get full too fast. It will also help you not to add too many calories to his daily requirement. Think about cutting his daily ration back a bit if you've had an extra-long training session.

Labrador Cross with ball

The reward is your dog's payback for playing this training game with you. It has to be something he's willing to work for, not simply something you want him to have. Some people have hang-ups about using food to train dogs because it cheapens their bond with the dog. They believe the dog should perform out of respect or love for them. Nonsense. Using food to train your dog is a way to get where you want to go. Training a dog with what he wants as a reward is both respectful to his doggy-ness and effective in the interest of time and resources.

Dogs don't perform out of love; their good behaviour or misbehaviour has nothing to do with their love for us. Even dogs that chew the couch and bite the postman love their owners. But if you want that postman-biter to like the postman, you'll probably have to use a reward that the dog likes a little more than a pat on the head.

Dogs are motivated by and will work for food, just like people work for money. We all need money to pay our bills and live our lives; dogs need food to live and enjoy theirs. Many dogs eat out of a bowl once or twice a day for free. Why not take that food and train the dog to behave in a way that is acceptable to you? Once a dog is hooked on training and you have a good bond with him, you can use other rewards to reinforce good or appropriate behaviour. Here are some ideas for treats:

· Boiled chicken
· Boiled beefburger
· Popcorn (unsweetened)
· Tortellini or other types of pasta (cooked)
· Bread (bagel pieces work well)
· Carrots
· Bananas or apples
· Dried fruit
· Cheese
· Freeze-dried liver (found in pet stores and supply catalogues)
· Sausages (cooked)

How does *random reinforcement* work?
Once your dog has mastered new tricks, start giving him treats sporadically. He won't know for certain whether he's getting a reward, but he probably won't take the chance of missing one, either.

To prevent your dog from getting diarrhoea, don't give too much of any one thing. As your dog starts to like the training game, mix in less desirable treats (such as dog food) with the yummy stuff so that he never knows what he is getting. Random reinforcement will keep him more interested in the game, and should let you accomplish more in each training session.

Other Rewards

Most of the time we use a food reward in training because it is quick and easy. In beginner classes especially, students use treats because there is a lot to accomplish in only one hour a week. If yours is a dog that gets excited over tennis balls or stuffed toys, or he likes Frisbees or chasing a torch beam, use these rewards paired with the click (see Chapter 4).

Toys and games are a whole different category of rewards that may be exciting to your dog. If you find that your dog likes games and toys, make your training sessions even more exciting by mixing them in with food rewards. Some sessions could be all-food rewards or all toys and games, or you can mix it up and see what elicits the best response. When using toys as a reward, the key is to make the play part brief and fun. The game might last 5–10 seconds, and then the toy gets hidden and you get back to work. That way the reward doesn't distract the dog from the lesson. Here are some ideas for non-food rewards:

- A short game of fetch
- A short game of tug
- A short game of catch
- Hide a toy and find it together
- A toss of a Frisbee
- Chase a stream of bubbles
- Lots of happy praise and baby talk
- Vigorous petting and happy talk
- Torch tag (get your dog to chase the light beam)
- A stuffed dog toy
- A stuffed dog toy that makes noise
- A squeaky toy with an obnoxious squeaker

Dogs are affectionate animals, and any time you spend praising them and showering them with attention is time well spent. The chances are that you'll get as much from the affection and exercise as they do!

Help Your Dog Like Other Rewards

Some dogs love toys and will happily work for a toss of the ball, at least for part of the time. Dogs who are not as crazy about toys can learn to like them if you work at it. It is worth the effort on your part to get the dog interested in varied rewards, because the more he finds rewarding the easier it will be for you, and the more effective your sessions will be. Here's how to get started:

1. Hold your dog on a lead and tease him with a toy.
2. Throw the toy out of range and ignore his struggles towards it, but don't let him get it.
3. Use a helper to make the toy more exciting if necessary.
4. Wait patiently until the dog looks away from the toy and back at you.
5. Mark that moment with a click and allow him to go and play with the toy as the reward (see Chapter 4).
6. If he doesn't turn away from the toy in about 30 seconds, slowly go backwards to increase the distance between the dog and the toy. Click and release him to get the toy when your dog looks back at you.
7. Repeat this with different toys, and allow the dog to play with the helper every once in a while.
8. The play part of the reward should be brief, about 10 seconds.

This exercise should help you gee up a dog that is only mildly interested in toys. Warming him up this way is often a great way to start a training session – it helps the dog realize that it's time to work.

Exciting rewards are critical to an effective programme. If your dog isn't turning himself inside out for the reward, find something he likes better. Don't worry if you just can't get your dog interested in toys; there is no crime in using food in training. Remember that your dog eats for free every day, so it's acceptable to make him work for it instead.

Reward or Bribe?

Using food to teach your dog to perform tricks is simple, fun and effective. One problem that many people complain about, however, is that in the absence of food the dog won't perform. That just means that you aren't there yet. If you use food correctly, you won't need to use it to get the dog to perform the trick; it will come after the trick has been performed. This is the critical difference between a reward and a bribe.

A bribe is something that causes a reaction to happen by enticing the dog. For example, your dog is out in the garden and won't come in, so you shake a box of biscuits to bribe him in. This isn't really a bad thing, but it isn't training either. Bribing can have its benefits, however, when you are in a hurry and out of options.

Be aware of the difference between bribes and rewards; they can mean the difference between a well-managed dog, whose behaviour is dependent upon your attentiveness and his hunger level, and the well-*trained* dog that responds to cues immediately and reliably because he knows that the consequences will be good.

A reward, on the other hand, is something that occurs only after an action happens. A reward reinforces the likelihood that the behaviour will happen again. For instance, you call your dog at the park and he comes to you; you offer a treat and release him back to play again. A rewarded dog is far more likely to come to you the next time you call than is a dog that is put back on his lead and put in the car to go home. There are two types of rewards at work here: the food reward, which reinforced the dog for performing the action of coming back to his owner; and the consequence for coming back, which was that he got to play again.

If you know your dog well – his energy level, personality, special talents, limitations and motivations – you will be able to choose tricks that make both of you shine. Spend some time with your dog over the next few days and make notes on each of these categories. You may be surprised to learn how many things you assumed he would like that he actually doesn't. Adjusting your teaching style and training sessions can have a profound impact on the success of your training programme.

CHAPTER 3

Give Your Dog a Job

Most animals have a basic need for food, water and shelter, which we provide for our dogs with barely a second thought. The often overlooked needs that can mean the difference between a problem dog and a really great dog are exercise and mental stimulation.

Exercise First; Training Will Follow

Exercise is a crucial element in any training progràmme, and without enough of it, no real learning will occur. A dog without enough exercise is like a child without break time. What adult would like to teach a maths lesson to a classroom full of six-year-old children who haven't been outside to play all day? Without exercise, your dog will be hard to teach because he just can't be still long enough to pay attention.

Dogs vary in their exercise requirements, but all need at least 30 minutes of running, playing and interaction with you each day. The amount and type of exercise is dependent upon your dog's overall energy level. A Border Collie or active young Labrador will need one to two hours of flat-out running and active play, while a low-energy Pekingese may need only a 30-minute romp. Yet every dog is different, regardless of the breed and its stereotype. Ultimately, the amount of exercise your dog needs is whatever it takes to make him tired enough to be able to exist in your home as a calm, relaxed member of the family. Following are some clues that your dog isn't getting enough exercise:

· He paces from room to room in the house.
· He hardly ever lies down, even when everyone else is relaxed.
· He whines excessively for no apparent reason.
· He barks excessively, sometimes over nothing.
· He digs, destroys and chews everything in sight.
· He never stops jumping when there are people around.
· He runs away every chance he gets.
· He runs along the wall, using any excuse to bark at passers-by.

If your dog exhibits some or all of these symptoms, he could probably use more exercise and mental stimulation. Most people don't realize that leaving their dogs in the garden for hours at a time is not a good way to burn off energy, and not nearly enough exercise to make for a relaxed family pet. Most dogs, when left to their own devices, don't do anything but bark or dig or lie around.

If you are going to use your garden as a way to exercise your dog, you will need to go out with him and play games to burn off even a tenth of the energy he's got bottled up. Inviting neighbouring dogs over to play, if your dog gets along with them, might be another option. All-out running, chasing and wrestling are what a dog needs to do in order to be tired enough to be a good pet.

Energetic dogs that don't get enough exercise are obvious; they exhibit their excess energy in excessive barking, jumping and other unwanted behaviour. If your dog has behaviour problems, increasing the amount of exercise he gets can cut your training time in half.

Work Out Together

For dog owners with an active lifestyle, there are lots of ways a healthy active dog can burn off energy while accompanying you. Jogging, mountain biking and rollerblading are excellent ways to exercise dogs with boundless energy. Just make sure that you start off slowly and gradually build up the distance. In addition, pay attention to your dog's feet, checking them frequently for cuts and scrapes. Get him to him run on a variety of surfaces; pavement is hard on a dog's joints and bones.

Dogs that participate in such activities should be at least one year old and have been recently checked by their veterinarian for potential health problems. (Just as it can with people, vigorous exercise can exacerbate certain bone and joint disorders.) A fit dog is happier, and you will find that he is more focused on whatever activity you are enjoying together, and he will be more likely to do it longer and without injury.

Dog Sports and Activities

The reason we get a dog in the first place is to enjoy his company and share him with other people. Depending on your dog's personality and activity level, you may consider participating with your dog in any of a great variety of dog sports or activities. Enrolling your dog in an agility class might be an excellent way to introduce both of you to something new while maintaining a good level of fitness. Agility is an obstacle course for dogs involving things to climb over, around and through, as well as hurdles to jump over. The course is timed and dependent on you being able to successfully lead your dog through a maze of obstacles to the finish.

In this dog-friendly age of ours, services like reputable day kennels, dog walkers and obedience or ringcraft classes are available to help us exercise our restless pets. If you try to fit in more exercise sessions but just can't seem to put a dent in your dog's energy, consider a day kennel one or two days a week.

If you would like to be an active participant in your dog's exercise programme, you will find that there are many canine sports that require you to be almost as fit as your dog. From fly ball to tracking to search and rescue, the possibilities are endless. If your style is quieter, you may consider a visiting-therapy dog programme that allows you to go and visit a hospital or nursing home on a weekly or monthly basis. This is an excellent way to meet other dog owners and keep your dog's obedience skills sharp, because you will be using them constantly.

If you have a lot of free time and financial resources, you may consider becoming part of the search-and-rescue dog teams that look for missing people locally and nationally. No matter what your interest, there is a dog sport out there that you and your dog will both enjoy.

Games Dogs Play

Dog games are a great way to boost your pet's interest in learning new things and strengthen your bond with him at the same time. Regardless of the game, the true objective is to make sure you both have fun. Keep the rules simple and easy to follow, and play often. Involve as many people in the family as you can, and see how much fun it can be to learn new ways of interacting together. Consider the following activities and games:

Play Fetch – a great way to tire out a tireless Retriever. Use a tennis racquet to hit the ball that much further for all-out sprints.

Go swimming – another great way to exercise a very active dog. Combine it with some retrieving for a really exhausting workout.

Play hide-and-seek – an indoor rainy-day game may provide some dogs with enough activity to let them sleep the rest of the day. Also use this game to perk up your dog's memory and teach him that coming to you is always the best option.

Hide your dog's toys – he'll learn to use his nose to track things down *and* bring them back to you.

Learn a new trick – practise until it's perfect, then show off to your friends and family.

Practice Pavlov – set up a treat-dispensing toy, such as a Kong toy that can be filled with a few tasty treats. Show your dog how to interact with it until he manages to get a treat out of it.

Whatever you do, keep it fun, and keep the pace fast and interesting; you will see your dog perk up at the mere mention of playtime with you.

Provide the Right Foundation for Learning

Mental stimulation is the second-most overlooked need of problem dogs. Learning new things and solving problems make life interesting and give smart dogs something to do – and keeps them out of trouble, too! All dogs, regardless of breed or energy level, are intelligent and interactive creatures that love new experiences.

Dogs that are tied outside, constantly frustrated and emotionally neglected, may start off friendly and welcoming, but eventually become aggressive and wary of strangers. They have nothing to do, nothing to think about, and are absolutely bored. Dogs like this, even early in their adult lives (two to three years old), are hard to train. They aren't stupid or uncooperative, just blank. They simply do not know how to learn.

Lack of early stimulation and training makes it more difficult to teach any animal at a later date, because he doesn't know what to make out of the attention. It is possible to teach these dogs, but it takes patience, repetition and practice. The training methods and tools described in the succeeding chapters will help you teach your dog anything you care to take the time to teach.

Teach Your Dog to Think

The training methods described in this book teach your dog how to think and solve problems, which is important for any dog. The techniques are commonly referred to as 'clicker training', and are based in proven scientific theory. The rules and guidelines (see Chapter 4) will show you how to use this method to teach your dog anything physically possible. It is very exciting to see a dog grasp the concept of what you are trying to accomplish, and respond well without needing any corrections.

Golden Retriever holding keys

All puppies should attend a well-run puppy class that teaches you how to teach your dog the basic commands (Sit, Down, Stay, Come), how to walk without pulling and to come when called. The class should also offer a playtime for dogs in the 8–18-week range, and should be staff-supervised so that everyone has a good experience. It is crucial to the normal social development of your dog that he gets to play with other puppies and safe, well-socialized adult dogs on a regular basis. The more good experiences your young puppy has, the easier it will be to teach him anything later in life.

As you read and do research, you will find that there is no one way to train a dog. As your dog's primary caretaker, it is your job to find the methods that get the job done without harm to your relationship. Find a trainer who emphasizes building your relationship with your dog.

A list of qualities to look for in your dog-training class is as follows:

- A limited class size with an instructor/assistant-to-student ratio of 1:6 is ideal.
- The upper age range of the puppies accepted should be no older than 18 weeks.
- Handouts or homework sheets to explain exercises are important so that lessons can be shared among family members.
- The whole family should be welcome to attend. (If you include your children, make sure you bring along another adult to supervise them while you focus on training the dog.)
- All training methods should be positively based, ideally clicker training.
- Demonstrations should be given with untrained dogs to show the progression of exercises.
- Volunteers or assistants who help with the management of the class should be available to ensure that you get the help you need.

The best judge of a good puppy class, or any obedience class for that matter, is you. Ask if you can observe a class before signing up your puppy. Make sure the methods taught are kind and gentle, and that the puppies seem to be getting the message. Go with your first instincts – if you like the instructor and she seems like a person you can learn from, sign up. Train your dog; it's the nicest way to say you love him!

If a method makes you uncomfortable, don't do it. If you're not sure if something will work but the technique won't do any harm, go ahead and try it and see for yourself. Your dog will benefit greatly from an owner who is committed to finding the best way possible to train him to be the best companion he can be.

Practice and Consistency Are the Keys

As with anything in which you want to excel, the more you practise, the better at it you will become. All training is a learned skill; the more you work with your dog, the more effective you'll be as a trainer and as a team. For example, a beginning trainer may be notoriously stingy with rewards, and her timing may need some work. Through lots of practice, you will find and develop your own training style, discovering what works for you and expanding upon it.

Many resources are available, through books and online, that will tell you everything you'll ever want to know about behaviour and training. Search for obedience classes in your area, and keep at it. Remember that your dog and you are going to be together for a very long time – if you're lucky, maybe 10–12 years or even longer. Time spent teaching him how to learn will benefit both of you for years to come. Start your dog on the road to higher learning today!

CHAPTER 4

Clicker Training

Dog training has become kinder and gentler for both the dog and the owner. No longer is it necessary to use brute force or intimidation to force a dog to comply. Today, training any animal is about opening lines of communication and learning a common language. Clicker training isn't a gimmick or the latest fad; it is a solid, scientifically based technique that utilizes the positive principles of operant conditioning.

The Kindness Revolution in Dog Training

Use clicker training to teach your dog what you expect of him; it's an intelligent and overall time-saving exercise. Positive reinforcement through the use of treats and a clicker will help you teach your dog to think. The old style of training – making the dog 'obey' – is not only outdated, it also does not evolve his problem-solving skills or intelligence.

Training your dog with treats and a clicker is the fastest, most reliable, way to train your dog and have fun while you are doing it. There is no need to coerce, push or shove to get what you want; once your dog knows how to learn, you will have a willing partner and a better overall relationship. Many families have learned to train their dogs with a clicker and treats, and have enjoyed the learning process so much that they have come back again and again for more advanced classes.

Animals in zoos, aquariums and circuses have been trained operantly using positive reinforcement for decades. Can you picture putting a training collar on a killer whale and trying to make it jump? Just because you can force dogs to obey doesn't mean you should. Teach your dog to think instead!

The application of clicker training to dogs is pure genius; it simplifies and speeds up the process of learning for dogs and owners alike. Handlers of any age or size can learn the principles of clicker training, and because it is not dependent on corrections or physical manipulation, the size, strength and stamina of the handler don't matter.

Getting Started With a Clicker

The clicker is a small plastic box with a metal tab that makes a clicking sound when you push down with your thumb. The sound of the click is paired with a food reward by clicking the clicker and giving the dog a treat. After a few repetitions, the dog learns to associate the sound of the clicker with a food reward.

Why It Works

The click marks the desired behaviour to identify for the dog which action earned the reward. Because the food is removed by a step – you click first and then treat – you will find that your dog will work for the sound of the click rather than just a food reward. By pairing the clicker with a food reward, we have created a powerful way to communicate to our dogs what actions are rewardable. This comes in handy, especially with a very active dog, because it gives you a way to specify to the dog exactly which of his actions earned the reward.

tips

Starting with food rewards is faster than using toys and games. Once the dog begins to understand clicker training and how the game works, you can use other rewards, which can include balls, tug toys or playtime with other dogs.

Think of the click as a snapshot of what the dog is doing at the exact moment he is doing it. The click clearly identifies for the dog which action is being rewarded. Not only does this make it easier for the dog to understand what he is doing right, but it also gets him excited about the learning process, since it gives him the responsibility of making the click happen again.

The Clicker As an Event Marker

The sound of the click is unique, like nothing that the dog has ever heard, which is part of the key to its success in shaping behaviour. People often ask about using their voice instead of the clicker to mark the action they are looking for. In the initial stages of training, your voice is not a good event marker because you talk to your dog all the time, so your voice lacks the startling effect that the clicker invokes. The clicker's uniqueness reaches the part of the brain that is also responsible for the fight-or-flight response. In short, it really captures the dog's attention.

The process of shaping is what clicker training is all about. Shaping is useful in all types of training, but it is crucial in teaching tricks. Shaping behaviour helps the dog learn how to think about what he did to earn the reward. By not helping him or physically manipulating his body, you help your dog learn faster and more permanently by trial and error. Just like the jumping killer whale in the aquarium, clicking, or its absence, indicates which actions will be rewarded and which will not.

Once the dog has the idea that a treat follows each click, it is a good idea to remove the treats from your person and put them on a table, chair or step. The dog will still get the treat after being clicked for the right action, but the treat will no longer be in your hand or pocket. This exercise will teach your dog to pay attention to the click, not the presence of the treat.

Shaping

Shaping behaviour means breaking it down into steps that work towards an end goal. Shaping is not a rigid list of steps, but rather a general guide to get from point A to point B with lots of room for variation, intuition, rapid progress (missing steps) or reviewing if the steps are too big.

Prompted and Free Shaping

Shaping can be either prompted, using a food lure or target, or free-shaped. Free shaping requires waiting for the dog to offer desired actions on his own, then rewarding him with a treat in order to capture the small steps of behaviour that lead towards the end goal. Each trick you learn here will be broken down into its component parts. You can then embellish upon those steps if your dog needs things broken down further.

Training is not always a process that moves in one direction. Don't ever be afraid to stop a training session and go back to it later with a better plan and a fresh mind. Sometimes the best way for both of you to move forwards is to have a rest.

Keep notes on each trick you teach, and whether your dog is catching on to the components as presented or needs more explicit direction. You will find that detailed notes make it easy to pick up where you left off, and your training sessions will be more productive overall. You will reach your goals faster if you have a plan.

Free shaping is definitely worth adding to your bag of tricks in order to give you lots of options in explaining what you want your dog to do. You just show up with your clicker and treats, and click and treat what you like and ignore what you don't.

For training that involves natural talents or unusual actions, free shaping is the way to go. Because the dog is fully in charge of which actions he is offering, he will often learn faster (in some situations) and retain more than when you prompt his behaviour with a lure or target. Free shaping can be time-consuming, however, since it depends upon the dog offering the actions, and requires patience on the handler's part.

Working Through a Shaping Plan

Teaching a dog that likes to jump on guests to Sit instead is a lot more complicated than teaching just a Sit/Stay. The reason for this is due to all the distractions and variables during any given greeting. Though a dog may be able to Sit when there are no distractions, this doesn't mean he'll be able to Sit when a child with an ice-cream approaches him, or when he sees his favourite person. Dogs need to be taught how to Sit and Stay around gradually more stimulating distractions; they cannot automatically generalize their behaviour to suit all environments.

Teaching your dog to Sit instead of jumping requires that you break sitting down into small steps that are easy for the dog to accomplish, but at the same time introduce challenging distractions slowly so as to maintain the right behaviour. The steps to teach Sit/Stay around distractions are as follows:

1. Teach your dog to Sit by luring him with a treat, then clicking and treating him when his bottom touches the floor.
2. Once your dog is performing this well, delay the click by counting to two before you click and treat. This is the beginning of a mini-Stay.
3. Increase the amount of seconds between the time your dog sits and the click and treat, until your dog is holding the Sit position for 10 seconds at a time.
4. Once your dog can hold the Sit for 10 seconds between clicks and treats, go ahead and verbally label the action Stay, and include a hand signal if desired.
5. Help your dog generalize this action by going somewhere new or adding in distractions. You may have to lower your standards and start from the beginning until your dog learns to block out the distractions and pay attention to you instead.
6. Bring in people approaching your dog from the side and not making eye contact.
7. Bring in people approaching your dog from the front, looking at him.
8. Bring in people petting or talking to him.
9. Continue to change the variables until your dog will hold the Sit/Stay position regardless of the distraction.
10. As your dog starts to be able to handle the distractions and works longer and more consistently, wean him off the clicker and treats so that he will perform the action for the reward of being able to greet the person.

Dogs are not good at performing consistently; they don't automatically transfer an action to new or different surroundings. A dog will sit in the kitchen on the first command, but refuse to sit in a shop or the park. If you want to have control over your dog's behaviour, you should train him in all situations.

Using this shaping plan, you can teach your dog to sit, regardless of what is happening in the environment or who he is greeting. A less formal way to teach the same thing is listed below; you might try both shaping plans to see which one is more suited to your training style. The following shaping plan does not help the dog by luring him with a treat when he makes the wrong decision. Instead, this shaping sequence lets the dog make choices. You click only those choices that lead towards the goal of sitting and staying.

Often the dog may revert back to old habits, such as jumping and whining. Simply ignore the things you don't want and the dog will soon realize that those actions are not rewardable and will start paying attention to only the things he is being clicked for.

1. Start off by clicking and treating the dog for any action except jumping (standing, sitting, lying down, walking around) for the first minute.
2. In the second minute, choose something specific and click and treat him every time he does it. You'll want to pick something easy, such as standing still for one second or walking without whining, so that he can easily succeed.
3. If you have an active dog that does a lot of actions, you might want to limit his options by putting him on a lead and stepping on it so that jumping is not an option.
4. Continue working with the dog in short sessions until he starts to visibly startle at the sound of the click and holds the position for a second.
5. Next, withhold the click for a while and see what happens; most dogs will sit out of confusion and boredom, and you can click and treat that.
6. As soon as the dog sits (on his own without being prompted), click and treat.

7. Repeat this again and again, and gradually increase the amount of seconds the dog has to hold the Sit for a click and treat, until you have the dog holding the Sit for a reasonable amount of time.

8. You can continue on this way to polish the Sit to greet visitors in any way you wish.

Regardless of which shaping plan you choose, you will see that there are times when things will go fast and smoothly, and you may even miss out steps or make great leaps in your shaping plan. Other times you will come to a standstill as your dog gets muddled and confused about what he's supposed to do. You will need to re-evaluate your plan and break it down into further steps or help him out in some way. Learning how to shape behaviour will make you a better overall dog trainer and make training your dog more fun.

Tools of the trade: bit bag, clickers, lead and flat collar

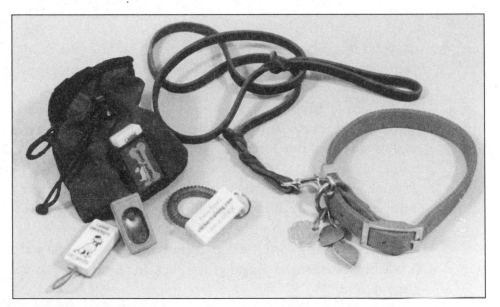

Using Lures in Training

A lure is a piece of food used to tempt your dog into performing. Its aim is to help the dog get into the right position in order to earn the click and treat. In beginning your career as a dog trainer, it is often frustrating and time-consuming to wait for your dog to perform the right action, so the use of a food lure gets things going. The problem with food lures is that unless they are dropped relatively quickly, the dog (and humans) become dependent upon them in order to perform the action. If lures are not dropped, you will not have a trained dog that can perform actions on cue; you will have a trained dog that follows food.

As a general rule, lure the dog six times in a row. On the seventh repetition, do all the same motions with your body, but without the food lure in your hand. If the dog performs the action correctly, click and treat. If he doesn't perform the action correctly, go back and lure him six more times and try it again. This mini-drilling session trains the dog how to perform the correct action, and it lets you see if he understands what he's being clicked for.

Do all dogs respond to lures?
For some dogs, lures present more of a distraction and a hindrance than help. For such dogs, you should ignore the lure altogether.

Your goal with using a food lure is to help the dog into position six times in a row; then on the seventh repetition, try hiding the lure to see if the dog starts to perform the action on his own. When you take the lure or treat out of your hand, you can start fading it gradually by putting it on a nearby table and running to get it after the click. The dog knows it's there and is excited about it, but is not dependent on you waving it around to get him into the right position.

Using this method to wean your dog off lures means that you get the dog to perform the action, click and then run to get the treat. Doing this exercise will help your dog to learn that he is working for the click, and that the treat is an afterthought.

Targeting

Targeting is a form of luring, but it removes the treat by a step. It involves teaching the dog to touch his nose to an object. You might use this tool in order to move your dog or get him to interact with someone or something. Anything can be used as a target, but the three main targets are your hand, the lid to a yogurt pot and a target stick. (You can make your own target stick out of a short piece of dowel; it helps if you paint the tip white.)

Hand Target

The idea behind using targeting is to get the action started but then wean the dog off the target so that he is performing the action reliably without it. The same rules apply to weaning off the target as to weaning off the lure; use it to get the action started and then wean your dog off it. To teach your dog to target your hand with his nose, follow these steps:

1. Hold your hand palm up with a piece of food tucked under your thumb in the centre of your palm. Click and treat your dog for sniffing your hand.
2. Keep the food in your hand for six repetitions and then take the food out and repeat, clicking the dog for touching his nose to your palm.
3. Get the dog to follow your hand in all directions while you move around the room.
4. Involve a helper and get your dog to target your hand and then your helper's hand for clicks and treats.
5. Name the action of touching his nose to your hand by saying 'Touch'. (More on naming follows.)
6. Try the trick in new places and with new people until your dog is fluent. Don't be afraid to go back to using food for a few repetitions if your dog falls apart around a new distraction.

Lid Target

On occasion, you may want your dog to move away from you to perform an action at a distance. In that case, it may be useful for you to teach your dog to target a yogurt lid with his nose. The steps for teaching your dog to target a lid are listed opposite.

1. Put the lid in your hand and hold a treat in the centre of your palm with your thumb.
2. When your dog noses at it, click and treat. Repeat for six repetitions.
3. Present the lid with no treat and click and treat your dog for sniffing or nose bumping.
4. Name the action by saying 'Touch' again just before your dog touches the lid.
5. Put the lid on the floor close by and repeat, clicking your dog at first for moving towards the lid and then for actually touching it with his nose.
6. Move the lid at varying distances until you can send him across the room to bump it with his nose for a click and treat.

Stick Target

Another variation of targeting involves using a stick as your target. The target stick acts like an extension of your arm and is useful in working with your dog at a little distance from you. The steps for teaching your dog to touch a target stick with his nose are as follows:

1. Put the end of the stick in the palm of your hand with a treat, and click and treat your dog for sniffing or nudging at it with his nose.
2. Gradually work your hand up the stick, and only click and treat your dog for touching his nose close to the white end away from your hand.
3. Try putting the stick on the floor and only clicking and treating when your dog touches the ends.
4. Get your dog to follow the stick as you walk with him until he's racing to catch the end of it for a click and treat.

If your dog is doing a lot of mouthing of the stick, don't click until he does something more appropriate, such as nudging it with his nose. Be careful to click only appropriate touches, and ignore all others.

Paw Targeting

There may be times when you want your dog to interact with an object with his paw instead of his nose. Teaching your dog to target with his paw may give you another tool that you can use to help him learn whatever trick you are teaching. The difference between teaching your dog to target with his paw instead of his nose involves paying attention to which body part is hitting the target.

1. Put your hand or lid out for the dog to see, but withhold the click until he steps near it. Because you have already taught your dog to target with his nose, he may perform only this action at first. Be patient and wait for paw action near the target.
2. Withhold the click to let your dog know that you want something other than a nose touch, and see what happens.
3. Make it easy on your dog by moving the lid or your hand along the floor so that you can click him for moving towards it. An easy way to help your dog to get this action started is to put the lid at the base of the stairs and click him for stepping on or next to it.
4. When you withhold the click, your dog may get frustrated, but don't be too quick to help straight away; wait for your dog, and see if he'll paw at the target or move towards it.
5. Practise a paw target separately from a nose target, and make sure to have two distinctive cues for each one.
6. Frequent, short training sessions will help your dog work out what you want faster than long, confusing ones.

For targeting to be useful, you must practise it often. The more experience your dog has with this method, the better it will serve you in your trick training.

Naming Commands

The major difference between clicker training and other types of training is that you don't name the command immediately. The reason for this is that the early versions of the training are not what you want for the final command. The first click for heeling, for instance, is a far cry from what the finished action will be.

The command can come as a verbal cue or a hand signal or both, but should not be introduced until the dog understands what is required. If you name commands too soon, you will get a wide variety of responses from the dog. Wait until the performing looks close to perfect before naming the command.

Asking your dog to obey a command assumes that he knows what is required of him. The dog should obey the command (without clicking or treating or luring) 10 times in a row without any mistakes. If he doesn't have 100 per cent accuracy, do more training.

You can call each action or trick anything you want; just make sure that it is a simple one-syllable word as often as possible, and try to make sure that it doesn't sound too much like any other word you use with your dog. Dogs pick up a lot from your body language and the pitch of your voice but may have trouble distinguishing between similar-sounding words, such as *no* and *go*, for instance.

Weaning off the Clicker and Treats

The clicker is a learning tool, a signal that identifies for the dog which actions will be rewarded. When the dog is performing the action on cue and reliably (with 100 per cent accuracy), he is ready to be weaned off the clicker and treats.

One way to begin the weaning process is to get the dog to repeat the action more than once before you click and treat. This gives the dog the idea that he must continue to perform the action until he hears his click. The worst thing you can do when you are weaning your dog off the clicker and treats is to do it suddenly and abruptly. Getting rid of rewards and affirmation that he is performing the behaviour correctly all at once is too harsh, and will result in a frustrated dog.

The key to weaning is going slowly, getting the dog to perform longer versions of the action, or performing it in more repetitions successfully. The weaning process may be a good time to start introducing non-food rewards, such as the opportunity to greet a guest after sitting, or being released to play with other dogs after coming when called.

The Last Word on Using Food

Eating is most dogs' greatest joy, a pleasure that you can use to help your dog learn appropriate manners and become a well-behaved member of your family. Regardless of a dog's preference for particular types of food, all dogs need to eat in order to survive. So, whether your dog is food-orientated or not, every dog will work for food – you may just need to search a bit to find the right kind. What instructors love about clicker training is that it works for every dog.

Don't use fattening dog biscuits as treats. When it comes to calories, one dog biscuit is like eating a snack-size chocolate bar. Instead, use things such as carrot sticks or soft dog treats cut into small pieces.

Clicker training is successful because the emphasis is on the click, not the treat. Once dogs work out the game, they love it and will gladly work, regardless of how they feel about food. If you have a finicky fellow, try diversifying what you use as the reward and cutting back a little on his daily meal.

For dogs that like to eat, you may have the opposite problem: too many calories. Clicker training uses a lot of food rewards, but that doesn't mean that you'll necessarily have a fat dog. The size of the rewards should be tiny, 6mm ($^{1}/_{4}$in) or less, and can even consist of the dog's meals.

Golden Retriever waving

If you have a particularly long training session, you can feed less food at the next meal or use the actual meal to train. The length of your sessions should be 5–10 minutes maximum, so your dog is not going to be getting a lot of extra treats at one time. If your dog is on a special diet, consult your vet and find out what food treats you can use.

The beauty of clicker training is that it teaches dogs to think. It is a kind, non-violent way to teach a dog what is expected of him. It is also long-lasting and easy, making it fun for the trainer and trainee alike. Enjoy using this method to teach your dog anything your heart desires, starting with some of the coolest tricks around.

CHAPTER 5

Dog Training Basics

The time you spend training your dog is critical to developing and fostering a relationship with him. Training in itself is a relationship because of the way you communicate with your dog and develop a common language of words and signals. Dogs that are trained to respond to basic commands are more fun to own because you can direct their behaviour for a more enjoyable life together.

Invest in the Future

An untrained dog still learns things – just not necessarily the things you want him to know. Part of your dog's training and communication skills has to do with the structure you provide for him about what is and is not allowed. Putting in the time to teach your dog the basics around various distractions and in new environments is part of being a good dog owner, and will help you avoid future behaviour problems. The better trained your dog is, the better relationship the two of you will share.

Leadership Involves Controlling Resources

Dogs are pack animals; they thrive on rules, consistency and expectations. Setting limits about what is allowed and how you expect them to act is not only fair, but essential to having a healthy, well-adjusted dog. Don't worry! Being a strong, fair leader is not about being physical with your dog. A true leader would never need to pin a dog down or give a harsh correction.

Leadership isn't about forcing dogs to obey. It requires you to provide structure and establish boundaries by controlling resources. The amount of time you spend establishing that you are the greatest person in your dog's life, the one who has the ability to give your dog access to all that is important to him, the more control you will have over your dog's behaviour and the better behaved he will be.

Leadership is about controlling access to the things your dog wants, including sleeping and resting places, food, toys, attention, access to other dogs, or access to the outdoors. It is ultimately about *you* being in command, not the dog.

The relationship between a well-behaved dog and his owner is one that consists of limits and rules about what is expected, as well as consistent training so the dog can recognize what is expected. Developing a relationship through training will mean that you will always have a way to communicate with your dog and nip behaviour problems in the bud or avoid them altogether. Being a strong leader is the first step towards ridding your dog of behaviour problems. Following are some guidelines on how to be a strong, fair leader.

1. Nothing in life is free. Make sure you give your dog a job. Make him Sit for dinner, Lie Down before doors are opened for him, etc.
2. Humans go first through doorways and up and down the stairs. This avoids escapes out of the front door or knocking you down the stairs. Teach your dog to Sit and Stay until he is released through the door.
3. Down/Stay sessions for 5–20 minutes at a time help teach your dog self-control and give him a constructive job to perform around distractions and company.
4. No dogs on the beds or furniture. Young dogs should sleep in a basket or their own bed, not in bed with you. Your bed is the highest, most special place in the house and should be reserved for you only.
5. Don't repeat a command more than once. If he doesn't respond on the first try, he does not get what you were offering.
6. Ignore your dog if he nudges you for attention. Leaders give attention on their own terms, not when their dogs demand it.
7. Ignore your dog if he is constantly pushing toys at you. Leaders initiate play and decide when the game starts and ends. This keeps a dog on his toes because he never knows when the fun begins.
8. Follow through. If you've asked your dog to do something but he does not respond, make sure you help him to get into the right position, rather than repeating the command.
9. Provide consequences. Ignore what you don't like; avoid yelling at your dog for barking or jumping, for instance. From your dog's perspective, any attention is better than none, and speaking to the dog can often be mistaken for reinforcement.
10. Avoid punishment. Instead, teach your dog what you want him to do.

Because you control the things your dog wants access to, your leadership will help you build a strong bond with your dog, convincing him that you are the key to everything he desires. Strong leadership will give you the foundation you need to teach your dog how to behave appropriately and become a welcomed member of the family.

The Ten Keys to Successful Training

Throughout this book, you will learn effective techniques to ensure the success of you as a trainer and your dog as a student. Most 'keys to success' are universal, but it will be helpful for you to think of them in terms of your pet.

1. **Be patient.** All dogs learn at different speeds and often don't grasp concepts as quickly as we think they should. Be patient with your dog, and help him to be successful.
2. **Plan ahead.** Set your dog up to succeed. If your dog isn't getting it, the action probably needs to be broken down into smaller steps.
3. **Be realistic.** Don't expect your dog to perform in an environment you haven't taught him in.
4. **Be kind.** Use positive methods to teach your dog what's expected of him.
5. **Avoid punishment.** Harsh corrections have no place in the learning phase of a dog's development.
6. **Reward effectively.** Reinforce proper behaviour with what motivates your dog. A pat on the head is nice but not necessarily what he wants. Remember that this is paytime: pay up!
7. **Be generous.** All new trainers tend to be cheap with rewards. Reward correct responses often, and don't be afraid to reward exceptionally good responses with extra treats, praise, toys and love.
8. **Set goals.** If you don't know where you are going and have not planned out the session, how will you know when your dog's got it?
9. **Practise often.** Teach your dog in short, frequent sessions.
10. **Stay positive.** Stop with your dog wanting more. An enthusiastic student is always an eager learner.

The simple truth of training dogs is that you get what you pay attention to. Set your dog up to succeed, limit his options and reinforce what's going right. Soon you'll have a well-behaved dog that everyone loves to have around.

Teaching the Basics

Basic obedience is part of most tricks. The better your dog's response to commands like Sit/Stay and Down/Stay, the easier it will be to teach any trick, especially the more complicated ones. The basics of Sit, Down, Stay and Come are the foundation material for most tricks covered in this book. If nothing else, having some knowledge of the basics will help your dog to relax enough to learn something new. Teaching your dog how to sit or lie down can help you position him for success. You can't just expect that working with your dog for a session or two will make him reliable around distractions and new people. If you want your dog to be well-behaved and respond to your commands consistently, you must put in the time to train your dog.

Teaching Sit

Teaching Sit involves luring the dog into position before you click and treat for the correct response. Remember that when using a lure, it's important to lessen its presence quickly to keep the dog from becoming dependent upon it (see Chapter 4). Removing a lure is an important part of making sure your dog becomes reliable, and is truly grasping the concept of sitting. The steps to teaching Sit are as follows:

1. Hold a treat slightly above your dog's nose and bring it back slowly over his head.
2. When your dog's bottom touches the ground, click and treat.
3. If your dog keeps backing away, practise against a wall so he can only go so far.
4. Repeat this until your dog is performing Sit readily.
5. Take the treat out of your hand and, holding your hand the same way, entice your dog to Sit. If he Sits, click and treat; if he doesn't, go back to using a food lure for six to eight more repetitions.
6. Once your dog is doing this reliably (follow the Ten in a Row rule), verbally name the command Sit immediately before the dog's bottom touches the ground.

7. Repeat these steps in various places until your dog is responding well with no mistakes.

8. Now, without a treat in your hand, ask your dog to repeat the action more than once before you click and treat. Start with low numbers of repetitions, such as two, three or four Sits before you click and treat, but don't follow a pattern.

9. To help him generalize the command, start practising somewhere new – the pet shop, the park, the vet's waiting room. Remember that forgetting is a normal part of learning and you will need to go back to helping the dog, with a treat in your hand if necessary, if the place in which you are working is very distracting.

10. To test your dog's training, try for ten in a row. If he gets less than 100 per cent, go back to practising before asking for the action in that environment.

If your dog fails the Ten in a Row rule, you need to help him for a few repetitions before he attempts the exercise again without help. Going back to the previous steps to help your dog get into the right position gives him information about what he needs to do to earn his click and treat and prevents him from getting confused and frustrated.

Teaching Sit/Stay

Miniature Pinscher being lured to sit

Turning the Sit into a Sit/Stay involves two processes: getting the dog to hold the position for longer periods of time (duration), and holding the position while the handler moves further away (distance). If you teach this action in two steps, you will have a reliable command that is resistant to falling apart around distractions. The steps for teaching duration include the following.

1. Get your dog into a Sit and then count to two before you click and treat.
2. Gradually increase the time the dog has to hold the position by several seconds before you click and treat until you can build it up to 10 seconds between each click and treat.
3. When you can get to 10 seconds, go ahead and verbally name it Stay and give the hand signal (most people use a flat open palm held towards the dog).
4. Increase the time between each click and treat randomly to keep the dog guessing as to how long he must wait for his next click.
5. Add in distractions, and start from the first step to rebuild the command of Sit/Stay around this new variable.

Try not to let your dog be wrong more than twice before helping him into the right position, lessening the distraction or changing the variables. If your dog makes more than two mistakes in a row, you need to change something so that he can be right more easily.

The second part of the Sit/Stay command is for the dog to hold the Sit while you move away from him. The steps for teaching your dog to hold his position relative to yours are:

1. Get your dog into a Sit and take a small step right or left, returning immediately. If your dog maintains his position, click and treat. If he doesn't, do a smaller movement.
2. Gradually shift your weight, leaving your hands in front of the dog. Click and treat the dog for maintaining its position in front of you. Practise this gradual movement until the dog is convinced he should stay in one spot.
3. Increase the distance slowly and keep moving at first, never staying in one spot too long without coming back to the dog to click and treat. Standing still too soon in the process will cause your dog to run to you.

4. As you are able to cross the room with your dog maintaining his position, start to stay away a few seconds longer before coming back.

5. Increase the time slowly so that you are combining both the length of time the dog holds the position (duration) and how close to, or far away, you are from the dog (distance).

Teaching Down/Stay

When you are teaching your dog to Lie Down and Stay there for extended periods of time, pay attention to the surface that you are asking him to lie on. Make sure it isn't extreme in temperature, and that it isn't so hard and uncomfortable that your dog fidgets and gets up a lot because it is too unpleasant to stay down. Short-haired dogs are often very uncomfortable on hardwood or linoleum floors, and will learn to lie down more readily on a carpet or towel.

1. Starting with your dog in the Sit position, use a treat to lure his nose about halfway to the floor. When your dog follows the treat by lowering his head, click and treat.

2. Gradually lower your hand closer to the floor. You may need to go back to a food lure for a few repetitions if your dog seems stuck and won't lower his head any further.

3. When you get the treat to the floor, experiment with holding it out under your hand, or closer to and under his chest, and wait. Most dogs will play around for a while trying to get the treat and then drop to the ground. When your dog goes all the way down, click and treat.

4. Repeat this six times with a treat, clicking and treating each time your dog goes all the way down.

5. Now, without a treat in your hand, make the same hand motion and click and treat your dog for any attempt to lie down.

6. If your dog fails more than twice, go back to using a treat for six more times and then try again.

7. Try this in other places. When you go somewhere new or involve distractions like other dogs and people, the action may fall apart a bit. Don't be afraid to go back to using a food lure to show the dog what

to do, and then fade it out when the dog is performing the action well and reliably.

Shetland Sheepdog puppy being lured into a down

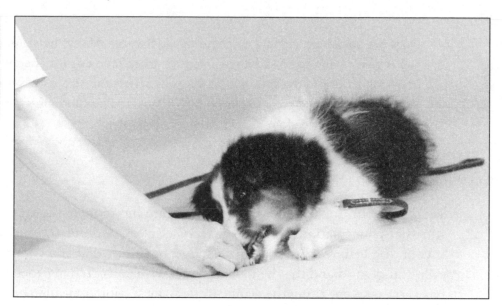

Some dogs have trouble lying down and seem to get stuck in the sitting position. Here are some tips for dogs that get stuck.

· Practise on a soft surface away from distractions at first.
· Use novel treats that the dog loves but hardly ever gets.
· Use a low table, the rung of a chair or even your outstretched leg to lure the dog low to the ground and under the object to give him the idea.
· Experiment with holding the treat closer to the dog's body and between the front paws close to the chest, or further away from his nose at a 45-degree angle.
· Avoid pushing on the dog to get him down. As soon as you start pushing and prodding, the dog turns his brain off and stops thinking about what he's doing, letting you do the work. If you want to teach your dog to think, don't push or pull him into position.

The most important thing to remember while training your dog, especially if you're struggling with a lesson, is to be patient and practise often. Short, frequent sessions will be much more effective for you and your dog than marathon sessions.

> Dogs are impulsive and love to chase things that run. Always be cautious about giving your dog freedom in unfenced areas. Your dog may be the best-trained dog in the area, but if a cat runs across the street he is likely to follow. Use a lead on all walks on busy roads, and be cautious when allowing off-lead freedom.

Teaching Your Dog to Come

Teaching your dog to come when you call him has more to do with the status of your relationship than anything else you've done to this point. If your dog believes that you are in charge, he knows that you control everything good and that he must interact with you often in order to have access to the things he wants. Review the section on leadership earlier in this chapter, and try to be diligent about becoming a strong and fair leader.

From a training perspective, the first thing a dog must do in order to Come is to turn away from what he wants and look back in your direction. To teach a strong foundation for Come, follow these steps:

1. Start with the dog on his lead in a slightly distracting area, keeping him from the things he wants, and wait for him to look back at you, then click and treat.
2. Repeat this until the dog no longer looks away from you.
3. Change the distraction, go somewhere more stimulating, or go closer to the distractions and repeat.
4. If your dog doesn't look back at you in 30 seconds or less, move further away from the distraction until he will look at you within that time.
5. When your dog is looking back at you predictably, run backwards as you click and deliver the treat at your feet to encourage the dog to catch you.

6. As your dog gets good at this, wait until he is on his way back to you before you click.
7. Verbally name this command Come as your dog gets to you to eat his treat.
8. Change the distractions. Increase the intensity of a distraction by going closer to it or increasing the distance between you and your dog by using a longer lead.
9. If your dog doesn't respond by looking back in a reasonable amount of time, don't be afraid to back away from the distraction.

The trick to teaching Come is to set your dog up to be successful. Don't allow off-lead freedom if your dog is not reliable, and practise, practise, practise! After establishing a firm foundation for Come on a 2m (6ft) lead, you would then use a longer lead and go back and review all of the steps from the beginning. Some dogs will make great progress quickly, and others will need you to go much slower so that they can be successful.

Gradually increase the length of the lead until your dog can turn away from what he wants (the foundation for coming when called) and come back to you easily. You would then progress to dropping the lead and letting him drag it, and eventually take it off while reviewing all the steps to teach Come. When you first take off the lead, you may want to practise in a fenced or protected area in case you've hurried your dog's training and he runs off and won't come. This means that you need to back away a few steps and put the lead back on for a while.

Although the process seems a bit long and tedious, it is well worth the effort of having a dog that comes reliably when you call it. As your dog gets good at checking in with you, you can begin to offer real-life rewards mixed in with treats, such as the freedom to go back to playing with another dog, the opportunity to sniff a smelly spot on the ground, or the chance to chase a squirrel. If these opportunities are given as rewards, your dog will learn that coming to you and checking in on a regular basis is a very good thing. Regardless of how well your dog learns to come when called, however, remember never to allow him off-lead in unsafe areas where a mistake could cost him his life.

Minimizing the Cue

In early training, the original cue you use to get the dog to perform is overexaggerated. When the trick is polished, change the cue to something more subtle or change a verbal cue to a hand signal instead.

In order to change the original signal to a new one, the order in which you introduce the new command is very important. The standard practice for introducing a new command is: new cue followed by old cue. If you don't put the new cue first, the animal will ignore it and continue to respond to the old cue. You won't be able to get rid of the old signal unless the new signal precedes it.

Roll Over is a good example of a trick where you might want to abbreviate the original cue or replace it all together. When you first start the training, you'd probably use a full arm circle type of motion close to the dog's body to get him to throw himself over. You'd eventually want to shorten that to a slighter circular motion or even a closed fist.

To replace the old cue with the new one, you'll want to present the new cue immediately before the old exaggerated cue. Gradually make the exaggerated cue less exaggerated until the new cue is causing the action to happen.

Make a Plan and Chart Your Progress

Making a plan means breaking down each trick into individual steps and tracking or charting your dog's progress – and stumbling blocks. Get into the habit of examining your dog's success rate and periodically re-evaluate your shaping plan, making adjustments as necessary. Use the Ten in a Row rule as a general guide. If your dog can repeat a step with 100 per cent accuracy, you are ready to progress to the next step. If your dog makes a lots of mistakes or appears uninterested, break things down into smaller steps or change your approach in some way.

With each trick or action you teach, write each step down in sequential order and set small goals for each training session. Keeping your session short (less than 10 minutes) with a clear aim in mind will help you determine whether you need to make things easier for your dog. A training log is an important part of a successful programme, because your notes provide a bit of history on your progress. If you hit a snag along the way, you can review the steps where you were most successful, see what worked and make changes so you can keep moving forwards.

tips Whenever you are teaching a new action, click and treat your dog frequently. If you find that you are waiting around for some time for your dog to perform the right action, you need to break the command down into smaller steps. As you teach each new command, make sure that your dog has lots of opportunities to be right.

The Importance of Practice

Dogs learn things by repeating them over and over. The more you practise together, the better the dog will become at performing the action reliably and on cue. Dogs don't generalize well, meaning that just because they can Lie Down on the first try in the kitchen, doesn't mean they'll be able to Lie Down at the park or vet's waiting room.

The best way to ensure your dog's quick, reliable response to commands is to practise frequently in lots of different environments. The key to getting your dog to perform around distractions, such as people and other dogs, is to introduce them slowly. Give the dog as much help as he needs to be successful. Dogs don't need to be corrected for not performing an action in a new environment; they need to be shown what to do until they can perform the command on their own. If you find the need to correct your dog, you haven't done a good enough job of setting him up for success. Go back to the drawing board and plan out your sessions again.

Working on the Quality of the Trick

Working on the quality of the trick is an important part of taking your tricks to the next level. The qualities of distance, speed and duration will help you polish your tricks and let you expand them to more elaborate performances. Distance pertains to how far away from your dog you can be and still have him perform the trick; speed refers to how fast he can execute it; and duration indicates for just how long he'll hold a position.

> The simple truth of training dogs is that you get what you pay attention to. Set your dog up to succeed, limit his options and reinforce what's going right and you'll soon have a well-behaved dog that everyone loves to have around.

The key is to work on improving one aspect of your dog's performance at a time. For instance, if you want to teach your dog to wave to you at a distance, you would not ask him to hold the wave (duration) for any longer than he normally offers it. Similarly, you would not work him at a distance if you were trying to work on the duration of the wave. Separating these variables of trick training will help your dog learn faster, more consistently and more reliably.

Distance

To increase the amount of space between you and your dog, you simply need to lower your standards for all other aspects of the trick except his ability to perform it (however sloppily) at gradually increasing distances. Start with the dog close, and reinforce him for gradually increasing distances. You will know if you have gone too far because he will make mistakes. This means you should shorten the distance to where he was reliable and continue more slowly.

Once you have him working reliably at one distance, go ahead and gradually increase it until you are satisfied with the performance. Don't be afraid to go back to the beginning if your dog falls apart and you lose the action entirely. If you go back to the beginning and start again, your dog will catch on more rapidly and give you an even better performance.

Speed of Execution

Golden Retriever holding a beach spade

The speed at which your dog performs a trick refers to the time between the moment you give the command and the time the dog actually starts to perform the action. To improve your dog's speed, it is helpful to pick a number of seconds in which he has to perform the trick, and to reward only those repetitions that fall within your time limit. Anything more gets ignored. It takes most dogs only a short time to realize that it is how fast they perform the trick that counts. Don't forget that if you are working on the speed with which your dog responds to the command, you should lower your standards for other aspects of the trick.

What should you do if your dog refuses to perform a trick you think he knows?
If your dog does not respond to a command you think he knows, show him again, using a food lure or hand motion to help. Repeat this half a dozen times, and then try again. Dogs that don't respond to commands may be distracted by a new environment.

Duration

This aspect also refers to time, but deals with the amount of time the dog must hold the position, such as leaving his paw up to wave, before you reward him. You can teach duration by delaying the click for varying amounts of time and only rewarding repetitions that are longer than average. As you increase the duration, go slowly so as not to lose the action altogether. If you increase the duration too fast and the dog no longer performs the trick, go back to the beginning and start again. You will find that if you are flexible you will make an enormous amount of progress in a relatively short period of time.

Applying these tools as you go about teaching your dog any trick you choose will make it fun and interesting for your dog to learn. Concentrate on teaching the basics using these common methods before you start teaching tricks. Having lots of options will make it more fun for you to train your dog, and more fun for him to learn what you want to teach him. If you follow the simple plan outlined in this chapter for establishing yourself as leader and teaching the basic commands of Sit/Stay, Down/Stay and Come, you will reap the rewards of a well-behaved member of your family.

CHAPTER 6

Nursery
Tricks

Teaching tricks does not need to be a complicated task. Even novice trainers can teach a dog an entertaining trick, giving both trainer and dog a sense of accomplishment. The tricks that follow are simple and easy to teach, and are appropriate even for puppies, with their limited understanding of the training game.

Teaching Simple Tricks

Each dog has a unique style of learning, and it is your job as his trainer to find the best techniques to explain to him whatever trick you are trying to teach. The number of sessions necessary to learn one trick will vary according to the dog, so know that as long as you are progressing from one step to the next, you are succeeding. Some additional things to keep in mind as you work on new tricks with your dog:

- Only introduce one new skill per session. Skipping around too much will confuse the dog, and might discourage sensitive dogs altogether.
- Remember that the shaping outlines are building blocks towards an end goal. As with most goals, teaching a trick is accomplished by starting at the beginning with the first step and progressing through to the end by adding each step, one at a time, until all the steps come together to form a trick.
- Once you've established a few basics, it's a good idea to review previous skills or steps as a warm-up.
- Try to work in two or three sessions per day to see real improvement and accomplishment in a week's time. There should be at least two hours between sessions. Dogs take time to process what they have learned, and sometimes a rest gives them time to put more challenging concepts together.

You can teach the following tricks most easily using one of the three tools mentioned in Chapter 4 – luring, free shaping or targeting. You may want to review the basics often to reinforce your general skills before attempting to teach these tricks.

Polite Pawing

Many dogs can do these simple tricks with very little prompting because they already use their paws to play with toys or get your attention. If your dog falls into that category, teaching these tricks should be a fairly straightforward business.

Give Your Paw

Give Your Paw may be the most natural trick for dogs prone to pawing. However, it also serves as the foundation for other paw-orientated tricks, so master this one first. The shaping steps for teaching Give Your Paw are:

1. Find out what usually gets your dog to paw at you, and use it to get him to do it. As your dog's paw is in the air, click and treat.
2. Repeat this 15–20 times until your dog is offering his paw readily.
3. Now, leave your hand outstretched and wait for your dog; don't prompt him in any other way, and see what happens. If he lifts his paw at all, click and treat.
4. If after a few seconds he does not lift his paw, go back to helping him for another 10–15 repetitions before you try again. You want the dog to understand that the action of lifting his paw is what gets the click and treat to happen.
5. If you are using your outstretched hand as the prompt that gets your dog to give his paw, this can be turned into the cue for the trick. Show your hand, and click and treat your dog as he is stretching out his paw.
6. Add the verbal cue Give Your Paw when your dog is raising his paw to slap your hand on a regular basis.
7. Practise in different environments with various distractions, being careful not to overwhelm your dog. If the trick falls apart in the new place, don't be afraid to make things easier for him and help him out.
8. Avoid repeating yourself over and over; give one cue, wait for your dog's response, and click and treat. If your dog's response is not quick enough, go back to helping him for six to eight repetitions before trying again.

tips

If your dog does not usually raise his paw, try teasing him with a really tasty treat in your fist held at about nose height, scratching him on the chest or touching his toenails with your finger. Most dogs will respond by raising a paw, giving you an opportunity to click and treat.

High Five

The High Five is just a variation of the Give Your Paw trick with a few minor adjustments.

1. Teach your dog to target your hand with his paw for a click and treat (see Chapter 4).
2. Present your hand as the target in various positions until you can hold your hand up, palm facing the dog with fingers towards the ceiling. Click and treat your dog for touching your hand with his paw.
3. Practise this until your dog is quickly raising his paw when he sees you put your hand up.
4. Verbally name the trick High Five when it begins to happen on a regular basis.
5. Add distractions and work on getting him to do it with other people as well.

Sometimes you'll want to use a different cue or hand signal from the one you started with when you are teaching tricks. There is an order that must be followed before your dog will perform the trick on the new cue. You must take it one step at a time, or the dog will not pay attention to the new cue.

Wave

Teaching your dog to Wave is adorable and effective doggie PR because it gives him an appropriate way to greet people. Establishing an acceptable action, such as waving, is one of the keys to eliminating jumping. To perform this trick, the dog must raise a paw in the air while remaining stationary, which you can teach using a combination of targeting and shaping. The shaping steps are:

1. Start with your dog in a Sit/Stay and move a few steps away from him. Go back every few seconds for a full minute to reward your dog for not following you.

2. Standing in front of your dog, ask for his paw and click and treat him for giving it to you several times in a row.
3. Take a step away from your dog and ask for his paw. Click and treat the slightest effort to raise his paw without trying to move towards you. You may need to reward him for staying for a few repetitions before he'll remain in position and lift his paw.
4. As your dog raises his paw to place it in your outstretched hand, start removing this cue by removing your hand quickly. Click and treat your dog for hitting the air.
5. Repeat this step until your dog starts raising his paw when he sees your outstretched hand.
6. As your dog starts to offer his paw readily without moving forwards, you can begin to verbally name this new action Wave.
7. Change the hand signal to an actual wave by changing the position of your hand from an outstretched palm to a waving hand. Offer the new cue (the waving hand) right before the old cue (the outstretched hand), gradually removing the old cue until your dog is performing the trick when you are waving at him.
8. Add distractions and people, and practise in new places until the trick is reliable.

Calm Canines

Training involves many elements, but there are two things to remember. First, make the most of your dog's natural behaviour, as the paw tricks demonstrate. Second, use training to achieve desired behaviour, such as behaving in the presence of other people or dogs. The following tricks will help your dog remain calm, and will put your guests at ease as well.

Bow

Teaching your dog to Bow on command will not only make a flashy trick, but may also help you put a visiting dog at ease. Dogs invite each other to play in this position, and it can be an excellent way for your dog to learn to make friends. To perform this trick, the dog starts from a standing position and lowers the front half of its body until its elbows are touching the floor.

1. With your dog in a standing position, hold your hand below his chin (about 7.5cm/3in) and get him to touch your hand; click and treat.
2. Gradually make it harder by placing your hand closer to the ground by several centimetres each time. Click and treat your dog for making an attempt to lower his head further to touch your hand.
3. When your hand is resting on the ground, click and treat your dog for touching it with his nose without lying all the way down. If your dog continually lies down, raise your hand by several centimetres for a while before continuing on.
4. Make sure you watch your dog carefully, and click and treat any effort he makes to bend his elbows.
5. Once your dog will lower his top half, start giving him less help by removing your target hand before he touches it.
6. Decrease the hand target until he drops his head when you just begin to make the motion with your hand.
7. Increase the difficulty by only clicking and treating those repetitions where he lowers his head quickly.
8. Increase the difficulty by increasing the duration (length of time the dog holds the position) by adding a Hold It or Stay command. To increase the duration of the trick, delay the click by one or two seconds and gradually increase the time.
9. Add a verbal cue like Bow just before he performs the trick.
10. Try performing the trick in new places.

In order to make progress in trick training, you need to work at a pace where the dog is getting clicked and treated frequently. As you increase the difficulty of a trick, try not to let the dog make more than two or three mistakes before you show him what you want him to do.

Play Dead

Teaching your dog to Play Dead is a show-stopping trick that is sure to make even non-dog lovers sit up and take notice. This trick requires the dog to lay on his back with his paws in the air and hold it until released.

Shetland Sheepdog preparing to play dead

1. Get your dog to lie down, then click and treat.
2. Use a treat to roll your dog onto his side, then click and treat.
3. Decrease the lure by doing six repetitions in a row and then trying the seventh repetition without the lure, clicking and treating the dog for performing the trick.
4. Reintroduce the lure to get him to roll onto his back, then click and treat. Decrease the lure after the sixth repetition.
5. Go back and put all three steps together so that he performs them all in one continuous motion for one click and treat.
6. Decrease the lure by working with food for six repetitions then without food for two repetitions. Go back and forth until your dog responds with or without food. Note: the way you hold your hand will become the exaggerated cue that starts the trick.
7. Change the old cue to a new cue by offering the new cue before the motion you used to get the trick started.

8. Work on speed by rewarding the dog only for quick responses to the new signal. Decide on how many seconds he has to start the trick and click and treat even before he finishes. Clicking in the middle of the trick is what builds speed.

 Review Stay with your dog first; then gradually give the cue for the trick at greater and greater distances, only moving further away if the dog performs the trick reliably. Don't be afraid to do remedial work with Stay if the trick seems to fall apart.

Belly Up

This is similar to the Play Dead trick, except that it also involves allowing someone to touch the dog while he is flat on his back. Not all dogs are comfortable with this, so you should be sure you know your dog well before asking for it in front of strangers.

1. Get your dog to Lie Down, then click and treat.
2. Lure your dog onto his side, then click and treat.
3. Lure your dog over onto one hip, then click and treat.
4. Lure your dog all the way onto his back, then click and give a large number of small treats the first time, and stop the session.
5. Once your dog is rolling onto his back easily, decrease the lure after six repetitions and see what happens. If the dog performs the Belly Up trick, click and treat. If not, lure him six more times and try again.
6. When your dog is readily rolling onto his back, call it 'Belly Up' just before he performs the action.
7. Delay the click once your dog is in the Belly Up position by at first a few seconds and then more and more, until he will hold the position for longer periods of time.
8. Add in touching his belly, and click and treat him for holding the Belly Up position while you do this.

9. Add in the distraction of strangers touching his belly, and click and treat him for holding the Belly Up position while being petted.
10. Go out and practise the trick in new places with new people. Don't be afraid to help your dog into position if he gets confused in a new place.

Who Loves an Audience?

Although some of your training is behaviour modification, some of it is just plain fun. Once you've trained a well-behaved, socially acceptable dog, let everyone in on the games!

Roll Over

Roll Over requires your dog to lie down flat on his stomach, roll all the way over and get back on his feet. Though the concept is simple, this is not always an easy trick for your dog to perform. Long-back breeds, such as Dachshunds or Basset Hounds, may not be as good at this trick as other breeds, due to the way they are built.

Dogs with long backs sometimes find it uncomfortable and awkward to roll over on their backs and then try to get back on their feet. Overweight dogs or dogs that have had back injuries in the past may also have difficulties.

Pay close attention to your dog to be sure he's not hurting himself or twisting his back. If, despite your best efforts, your dog refuses to get on his back, don't push this trick; instead, try another one. Your dog may be sore or uncomfortable, and this may be his only way to express it. If possible, teach this trick on a soft surface, such as a towel or carpet, so the dog is more comfortable.

1. Get your dog to lie down with his belly touching the ground, and click and treat.

2. Use a treat or a toy to turn your dog's head until he flops over on one hip, and click and treat.

3. Use a treat or toy held close to your dog's shoulder to get him completely on his side, and click and treat.

4. Gradually move the treat or toy, while he's chewing on it, to move him onto his back and then eventually all the way over. This step often takes many attempts before the dog is comfortable enough to be on his back.

5. Click and treat small efforts to move towards the treat at first before you get him to move further to get his click and treat. If you make it too hard to earn a click, your dog will give up the trick and think it's no fun.

6. When your dog is rolling over easily, it's time to start decreasing all the extra cues and make him offer more before you click.

7. Once he can roll over with just this little bit of help, you can begin to verbally name this trick Roll Over. Whatever you are doing with your hand or fist could be a hand signal for the trick as well.

8. Add in distractions one at a time, and be prepared to help him complete the trick if he has trouble concentrating.

Spin

Spinning involves your dog turning in a complete circle in either direction. As your dog becomes good at this, you can get him to keep spinning until you tell him to stop. If you've tried to teach this trick using a lure or food treat, you probably realized how difficult it is to get rid of the lure. Instead, use targeting either with your hand or with a target stick to show your dog what you want him to do.

1. Use your hand as a target and, with your dog facing you, get him to follow your hand a quarter of the way around, then click and treat.

2. Now, leave your target hand at the quarter-way mark and wait until your dog touches it with his nose on his own before you click and treat. Practise this until he's offering it readily.

3. Next, just before he touches your hand, move your target hand to the halfway point and click and treat your dog for following it, but before he actually touches it.

4. At this point, as you drop your hand he may spin the rest of the way around, but continue to click and treat for the halfway point in order to build speed.

5. Use your target hand to start the dog turning, but then pull it away quickly. Click and treat your dog for attempting to turn without the target to guide him.

6. Time the click so that you're clicking the dog for being at the halfway point.

7. Continue to minimize your target hand and click the dog for continuing to turn without your help.

8. Decrease the target hand to just a motion to the left or right.

9. Lessen the target to a simple left or right cue. A pointed index finger would be appropriate as a final signal.

Once you and your dog have mastered this trick Ten in a Row, you can begin working on speed (see Chapter 5). Set a time limit in which your dog must perform the trick, and click and treat only those repetitions that meet the goal. To train your dog to spin in the other direction, simply go back to the first step and work your way through.

Are You Scared?

This trick will put a smile on everyone's faces, especially children's. To indicate his 'fright', the dog runs under a table or bed and peeps out from under the tablecloth or bedspread. The shaping steps for teaching Are You Scared? are:

1. Start with your dog under the table, and use your voice or a treat to get him to peep out. Click and treat.

2. Make sure you time your click for when he first pushes out from under the cloth.

3. Repeat this six to eight times, and then try putting him under again and waiting to see if he peeps out on his own.
4. Once your dog has learned this part, teach him to go under the table using a target lid (see Chapter 4 for teaching targeting with a lid).
5. Bait the target with a treat at first to encourage him to go under the tablecloth, and click and treat each time.
6. Take the bait off the target, but leave the target under the table or bed and send him again. Click and treat your dog for going under the table or bed after the target.
7. To get the peeping action, repeat the above step (getting him under the object) until your dog offers it readily, and then delay the click. When your dog doesn't hear the click, he will probably come back out to see what's wrong. Click and treat him just as he peeps out from under the cloth.
8. Repeat this until he runs under and peeps out each time; then verbally name the trick Are You Scared?

What if my dog doesn't peep?
If you're having trouble getting your dog to peep because he runs all the way out from under the tablecloth or bedspread, it means that you need to click sooner. An early click will catch the dog just as he is emerging and give him the idea that peeping is what is being clicked.

Who's a Brave Dog?

This trick is similar to Are You Scared? except that in this trick the dog runs around behind the handler and through his legs until he is looking up at the handler's face. The shaping steps to teach Who's a Brave Dog? are:

1. Starting with your dog sitting in front of you, use a target stick (see Chapter 4) to get your dog to go around you to the left or right.

2. Practise this until your dog will run behind your legs and touch the target for a click and treat.

3. Slowly move the target between your feet so that your dog comes between your legs enough to be able to look up at you.

4. Withhold the click after your dog starts to catch on to going through your legs and see if he will look up at you, then click and treat.

5. If your dog runs all the way through your legs, use the target stick to show him where to stop, and click and treat him before he actually touches it.

6. You can name this trick Who's a Brave Dog? by saying the name just before you give the cue that starts the trick, such as pointing or doing whatever you did to encourage the dog to go around you.

7. Slowly fade the target as your dog starts to perform the trick each time by showing the target to get him started and then making the target disappear.

8. Add distractions, and make sure to go back to helping your dog with the target stick if the trick falls apart.

Regardless of your dog's skill level, anyone can have fun teaching these simple tricks. Remember, the bottom line is to make sure you have

Boston Terrier targeting a target stick

fun while spending time with your best friend. Whether you teach your dog tricks to entertain your friends and family, or you do therapy work in hospitals and nursing homes, having a dog that can do tricks shows off all his amazing attributes. Spending time together learning something new will enhance your bond and strengthen your relationship, making the quality of life better for both of you. I hope you enjoy teaching these simple tricks, and I hope they inspire you to move on to the more complicated ones in the following chapters.

Social Graces

So your dog will shake hands and bow – that's clever! Well, you can certainly expand his social skills to include a few kisses and pleasant conversation. The joy of having a dog is your interaction with each other. These next two tricks really make the most of that.

Kiss Me

Teaching this trick utilizes a combination of free shaping and luring. You are catching the dog in the act of doing the action and rewarding it, but you are getting the action started by prompting it first. The shaping steps for teaching Kiss Me are:

1. Using food to excite your dog initially is the key. Feed him a few small pieces of a treat and eat a few yourself, then stick your chin out and wait.
2. At the first sign of any attempt to open his mouth to lick you, click and treat.
3. Try putting the treats in your mouth and showing him they're there. Click and treat any attempt to lick you.
4. Add the verbal cue Kiss just before you think he's going to perform the action. Click and treat as the action happens.
5. Show the food to the dog and put it away on a counter or table and command Kiss. When he kisses, click and treat and then go and get the treat.
6. Repeat this until the dog is beginning to offer the kiss as soon as you stick out your chin.

Experimenting with different types of rewards will make you a more versatile and successful dog trainer. Experiment with food rewards, games, toys and social opportunities (such as letting your dog say hello to a person after your dog performs Sit). Know where and when to use these to improve your dog's training programme.

Speak

Luring and free shaping, or a combination of the two, are the best tools for teaching this trick. The trick itself requires your dog to bark on cue.

1. Find something that causes your dog to bark, such a knock on the door or holding a treat out of range. Click and treat him when he barks.
2. Repeat at least 20–25 times.
3. Lessen the antecedent to barking (the knock), and if your dog starts to bark, click and treat.
4. Verbally name the action Speak just before your dog barks.
5. Don't click and treat for any barking other than the one you ask for.
6. If he barks at inappropriate times, be obvious about turning your upper body away to let him know that extraneous barking will not be rewarded.

After basic obedience training skills (Sit, Stay and Come), these simple tricks are the best opportunity for you and your dog to build a trusting and cooperative relationship. You'll develop a better understanding of how your dog thinks and what motivates him, and your dog will learn to read your cues. Take the time to train your dog well – you'll both get the best results that way.

CHAPTER 7

Retrieving Tricks

Any dog can learn to pick something up in his mouth and bring it to his handler. Although some dogs have an instinctive talent for doing this, even the most reluctant dog can learn to retrieve using operant conditioning by means of a clicker and treats.

Shaping the Retrieve

To shape the process of retrieving, break it down into tiny increments. Even dogs that are retrieving fanatics may refuse to pick up certain objects such as keys or tools. Teaching a shaped retrieve using operant conditioning will not only make your dog a reliable retriever, it will also give you a strong base for teaching the retrieving tricks that follow.

When shaping a dog to retrieve, it is best to pick an easy object to start with, something the dog is likely to pick up on his own. If you're not sure what texture appeals to your dog, set out a number of objects and see which he chooses to play with on his own. Most dogs don't like to pick up metal and have difficulty picking up small objects that require them to push their nose into the floor trying to get their mouth around it. Choose something your dog can get his mouth around easily, such as a face cloth, a retrieving dumbbell or a small empty box.

When you are training for retrieving exercises, use an object that you can put away when the session is over. Keep the item 'special' so that your dog looks forward to working with it every time you practise.

Using a new object will make it more likely that your dog will at least investigate it, giving you a starting point for shaping the retrieve. Teach the retrieve by breaking it down into the most basic steps so that it will be resistant to falling apart later. The shaping steps to teach the retrieve are as follows:

1. Put an item on the floor about 1m (3ft) away from your dog.
2. Click and treat him for moving towards it.
3. Click and treat him for touching the object with his nose.
4. Repeat this step about a dozen times, and then withhold the click.
5. If he mouths the object at all, click and treat.
6. Once your dog is mouthing the object, withhold the click until he picks up the object.

7. Delay the click again, and build up the time he will hold the object.
8. Add distance by putting the object a short distance away at first and gradually increasing it.
9. Name the retrieve Take It as the dog is picking up the object.
10. Name the release of the object Give or Leave It.

Wait for your dog to get frustrated enough to actually close his mouth on the object before you click and treat. More than likely he will mouth the object quickly and release it, so be ready to click and give a treat.

Links and Chains

As tricks become more complicated, you realize that one command really represents several actions – a training chain. In training your dog to perform these more complicated tasks, you can use two approaches: the training chain or back-chaining. Really, the only difference is whether you start with first things first or work your way backwards from a successful conclusion.

Training Chains

The concept of a training chain is relatively simple. In order for your dog to bring his lead to you on the command of Fetch Your Lead, he must: know where to find the lead; take it in his mouth (which may mean picking it up off the floor or pulling it from a doorknob); carry it to you in his mouth; and release it into your hand. Each of these steps is a link in the training chain, which is only as strong as its weakest element.

If your dog doesn't know how to carry objects without a lot of extra commands and prompting, training chain tricks will be difficult and uninteresting. Breaking things down into their component parts is a way of simplifying the trick and improving your dog's performance of it. A training chain is simply the breakdown of what the dog has to do in order to complete the command.

Back-Chaining

Back-chaining is related to training chains, except instead of training step 1, step 2, step 3, you train it backwards: step 3, step 2, step 1. The idea is that if you train something backwards your dog will perform the trick more reliably and with greater speed and enthusiasm because he is moving towards something he already knows well. By teaching him a multi-step task backwards, you are helping him remember the steps more easily because he learned the last one first. So, in the case of the trick Fetch Your Lead, it would be: hold the lead and release it into my hand; carry the lead to me from a distance; take it in your mouth; find it.

If you come across an object that your dog refuses to retrieve, go back and reshape the retrieve using this object. If the retrieving part of the trick is weak because the dog is not comfortable retrieving this particular object, the performance of the trick will become sloppy and unreliable.

Each of these steps may need to be broken down further to meet your dog's individual needs, but the basic concept is the same. When the dog performs the whole trick, he will be moving from less familiar steps to more familiar steps. Because he learned the last part of the trick first, he will be more confident and flashy as he gets to the end, and more reliable overall in his performance of the trick.

The Retrieving Tricks

Each of these tricks involves the dog retrieving or picking up something in its mouth and transferring it to another person. If your dog has any difficulty picking up the prop you are using, don't be afraid to go back to the basics steps of the retrieve using the new object. You will find that going back to the basics will help your dog's overall grasp of retrieving, and will make him less likely to refuse to cooperate.

Fetch Your Lead

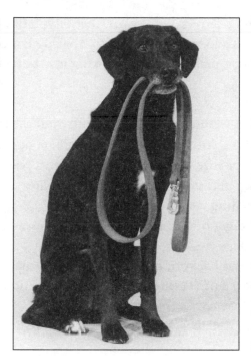

Labrador Cross holding his lead

This trick involves getting your dog to retrieve his lead and bring it to you. To make this easier on the dog, you may want to have one place where you leave your dog's lead, such as on a doorknob or by the front door. The dog has to go to where the lead is kept and pull the lead off with his mouth. He needs to carry the lead to you and hold it until you take it from him.

If you teach this and the following tricks using back-chaining, you will find it easier for your dog to perform them because he is always moving towards the more familiar steps.

1. Hold the lead out and ask your dog to take it. Click and treat the exact moment he puts it in his mouth.
2. Go back a step and see if he will follow you; click and treat him for moving with the lead in his mouth.
3. Put the lead on the floor and tell him to Take It. As soon as he picks it up, click and treat.
4. Put the lead on the floor, but don't click and treat until he takes it and takes several steps towards you.
5. Put the lead in various places at various distances and repeat. Click and treat for taking it under these new circumstances.
6. Gradually move the lead to where your dog can expect to find it, and click and treat him for going to that spot.
7. Replace the Take It cue with Lead, by saying the new cue Lead just before the old cue. Gradually decrease Take It so that your dog will perform the trick on the new cue.

Get the Post/Newspaper

This trick works well if you have a letterbox for your post or you have a daily newspaper delivered to your door. For this trick, your dog has to go to where the post or paper is kept, pick up the item, bring it to you and release it into your hand.

1. Teach your dog to carry non-essential letters and junk mail without stopping to shred them before you use the real thing. ('The dog ate the mortgage statement' probably won't go down well with your partner.) Do this by clicking and treating your dog for taking the letter or newspaper and holding it without mouthing it.
2. Take a step or two away and get him to bring it to you. Click and treat the motion of moving towards you.
3. Put the letter on the floor and tell your dog to Take It. You may want to use junk mail for this part until your dog refines his techniques for picking up something so close to the floor.
4. When your dog is retrieving well, begin to work him with the real post pile or newspaper.
5. Name this trick Post or Paper by saying this new cue just before the current cue Take It; pretty soon your dog will be fetching with enthusiasm and style.

Performing retrieving tricks in public can prove difficult; if you practise in different locations from the very beginning, your dog will be comfortable retrieving anywhere.

Find the Remote

Visitors, especially those with only a mild interest in dogs, love this trick – guests are always impressed when a dog can serve a useful purpose. If one of your household tends to hog the remote control, your dog can be your accomplice in getting it back with a smile. For this trick, the dog has to find the remote, pick it up, carry it to you and drop it into your hand.

1. Hand your dog the remote and click and treat him for holding it.
2. Back away a step or two, and click and treat him for carrying it to you.
3. Put the remote on the sofa or coffee table, and tell your dog to Take It. Click and treat him for picking it up in his mouth.
4. Send him into the living room at greater distances, and click and treat him when he finds the remote.
5. Call him to you as he gets the hang of this, and click and treat him for holding it until you reach out to take it.
6. Replace Take It with the command Remote by offering the new cue immediately before the old cue.

Fetch the Phone

Nothing is better than having your own personal answering service. For this trick, your dog has to go and retrieve the phone and bring it back to you. You may want to use a cordless phone for this (unless you sit close by) and store it on a low table or the floor to make it easy for your dog to reach it.

1. Hand your dog the receiver, and tell him to Take It. Click and treat your dog for taking it in his mouth and holding it for a few seconds.
2. Hand your dog the phone and back away from him, encouraging him to follow you. Click and treat him for carrying the phone to you. Make sure the click happens while he is moving towards you, not when he arrives.
3. Repeat this step again, but now click and treat your dog for delivering the phone to you.
4. Put the phone on the floor and ask him to Take It; click and treat him for picking up the phone.
5. Put the phone at greater distances and get him to retrieve it from further away. Time the click and treat for when your dog puts his mouth on the phone.
6. Increase the difficulty by delaying the click until he has the phone and is turning back to you. You can use a voice prompt like his name or the Come command.

7. Name the trick Fetch the Phone by saying it just before the commands Take It and Come, until you can gradually decrease the old commands and replace them with the new command.
8. Practise in short sessions until your dog begins to move towards the phone on the command Fetch the Phone.

Using a cordless phone for this trick is ideal; however, you may want to start practising with the receiver from an old phone to prevent damage to your existing one. Once the dog is good at picking up the receiver without damaging it, make sure you make the real thing easily accessible to prevent him dropping it or knocking it off the table.

Get Your Dish

Golden Retriever holding his dinner bowl

This trick is a great way to show off your dog's intelligence. You'll probably want to keep his food dish in one spot so that he knows where to go to get it. For this trick, your dog goes and brings his empty dish to you. Some dogs find it hard to retrieve metal dishes, in which case you may want to use a plastic one instead. If you decide to use the metal dish, don't be afraid to review the retrieving steps with this new object. The shaping steps for this trick are as follows:

1. Hand your dog his dish and tell him to Take It. Click and treat him for holding the dish.
2. Take a step away and call him to you. Click and treat him for moving towards you with the dish in his mouth.

3. Put the dish on the floor and tell him to Take It; click and treat him for picking up the dish.
4. Now repeat this step, but back away and click and treat the dog for picking up the dish and moving towards you.
5. Put the dish closer and closer to where you normally keep it, and send him to take it over greater distances.
6. As your dog gets better at this, replace Take It with the new verbal cue Get Your Dish by saying the new cue immediately before the old cue, until the dog starts the trick on the new cue.

> Some dogs hate having anything metal in their mouths. For these dogs, you may want to go back to nursery school and re-teach a retrieve with a metal object. See the shaping steps for teaching the retrieve, and substitute the object for the metal bowl.

Find My Keys, Please

If you are a person who constantly loses your keys, this trick may save you a lot of time. For this trick your dog has to locate your keys by using his eyes and sense of smell, pick them up, bring them to you and release them to your outstretched hand. The shaping steps are as follows:

1. Hand your dog your keys and tell him to Take It. Click and treat him for holding your keys.
2. Take a few steps back and call him to you. Click and treat him for moving towards you with the keys in his mouth.
3. Put the keys on the floor and tell him to Take It; click and treat him for picking up the keys.
4. Repeat the previous step but back away, and click and treat him for picking up the keys and moving towards you.
5. Put the keys in different places at varying distances, and click and treat your dog for finding them. Vary where you put them, sometimes leaving them out in the open, sometimes leaving them concealed.
6. Gradually work it so that your dog is actively searching for your keys. When you are at this point, name the trick Keys. Replace Take It by

giving the new cue immediately before the old cue. Then gradually decrease the old cue.

7. Practise this one frequently to keep your dog motivated about searching for your keys.

Delivery Tricks

The fundamental skill involved in retrieval tricks is the dog's ability to carry things in his mouth. The secondary skill is the dog's ability to carry things in his mouth from one place to another. Delivery tricks simply change the 'from' and 'to', which, as these next few tricks will show, can be fun *and* functional.

Put Away Your Toys

This trick will impress your more practical non-dog-owning friends. A dog that picks up his own toys beats a partner or child who can't find the laundry basket or put the dirty dishes in the sink. For this trick, the dog has to pick up one toy at a time and put it in his toy box or basket. The shaping steps are as follows:

1. Hand your dog a toy and tell him to Take It; when he has the toy in his mouth, click and treat him for holding it.
2. Put the toy box between your feet and encourage the dog to come to you; click and treat him for holding the toy over the top of the box.
3. Repeat the above step, but ask the dog to Leave It as he holds the toy over the box.
4. Put the toy on the floor and tell him to Take It; click and treat him for picking up the toy.
5. Repeat the above step with more than one toy on the floor at a time.
6. Replace the Take It and Leave It cues with the new cue Toys Away by saying the new cue immediately before the old cue. Gradually decrease the old cue.

Bring This to Me

This trick is great for dogs looking for a job to do. Having your very own canine delivery service is a great way for your dog to earn his keep. For this trick your dog has to pick up an object – a note, a tool or any item that is reasonable for him to carry – and take it to someone else in the house. The shaping steps are as follows:

1. Hand your dog an object, using the command Take It, and get a helper to call him from a step or two away. Click and treat him for moving towards that person.
2. Gradually move the helper further and further away, and click and treat the dog for moving away from you and towards your helper.
3. Gradually decrease the helper calling the dog, getting the person to go out of sight.
4. Replace the Take It command with Bring This to Me, by saying the new cue right before you say Take It. Click and treat the dog for taking the object and moving in the direction of the helper. Gradually reduce the old cue.
5. Vary the objects you get the dog to carry, and practise often. This is the type of trick that gets better the more you practise it.

Being a good dog trainer involves good planning. Trainers who plan ahead and map out their training sessions tend to have more success than those who don't. Clear targets and clear steps for reaching them are essential to knowing when your dog has arrived!

Post a Letter

Teaching your dog to post a letter is a fun and functional trick that uses lots of energy and is pretty entertaining to watch. Your dog must take a letter in his mouth, jump up against the postbox, and push the letter through the slot.

This trick can only be taught to dogs that are tall enough to reach the top of the postbox, unless you give a little one a boost. The shaping steps for teaching this trick are as follows:

1. Using the Touch command, ask your dog to use his nose to push the letter into the slot. Click and treat him for touching his nose to the letter.
2. Withhold the click and treat until he pushes the letter a little further towards the slot this time.
3. Get him to put two front paws on the postbox, and click and treat him for staying up for gradually longer periods of time. If you have a small dog, you may want to hold him close to the box and click him for putting his feet on the box.
4. Hand your dog a letter and tell him to Take It. Click and treat him for taking the letter, then for holding the letter for longer periods of time.
5. Call him to put his paws on the box while holding the letter, and click and treat.
6. Work on this step until the dog is easily balancing on his hind legs while holding the letter.
7. Now try to get the dog to put the letter in the slot by telling him to Leave It and clicking and treating him for letting the letter go. You may need to hold small dogs close to the box.
8. Practise all the steps until the whole thing is fluid and the dog responds to your command Take It by following through with all the other steps.
9. Replace the cue Take It with the command cue Post It. Say the new cue just before the old cue, and gradually reduce the old one.

Throw This in the Bin

Teach your dog to pick up anything you point to, including drink cans or other household items. This retrieving trick requires your dog to pick up the rubbish and release the object into a rubbish bin. To make it easier for your dog to get the object into the container, you will probably want to use an open or swing-top waste bin that is no taller than your dog's elbows.

1. Work with your dog and get him to retrieve lots of different kinds of rubbish, and get him to bring the rubbish to you over increasingly longer distances.

2. Sit on a chair with the waste bin between your feet. Tell your dog to pick up an item, using the Take It cue, and call him to you; click and treat him when he is as close to the opening of the bin as he'll come.

3. Repeat this step, but delay the click by a few seconds until he is eventually standing with his chin over the edge of the bin.

4. With your dog standing close to the bin, tell him to Leave It, and click and treat him for releasing the rubbish. You will need to practise this so that your dog will eventually release the item into the waste bin.

5. Experiment by withholding the click until your dog makes a deliberate effort to drop the item into the bin.

6. Name the trick Throw It Away by saying this new cue immediately before the old cues Take It and Leave It. You will have to practise this many times before the new cue initiates the trick.

7. Practise with different items so that your dog will retrieve and discard just about anything you ask him to.

Consider the height of the waste or rubbish bin and its opening when you are teaching this trick. The height of the bin needs to be proportionate to the dog's head so the opening is easily accessible. As you add distance to this trick, you may want to weigh down the bin so that it doesn't tip over and scare the dog.

The Next Level

Just when you think you've covered just about everything, new games and tricks come along to keep you and your pet constantly learning together. You can play them in your back garden, at the beach, or in the living room. Your dog is part of your family; if he's well-trained and well-behaved, he'll be treated as such.

Let's Play Ring Toss

This old-fashioned game is a wonderful way to exercise a high-energy dog. For this trick, the dog has to pick up each ring and place it on the post one at a time. This routine is repeated until all three rings are on the post. You can buy a ring toss game inexpensively in any toy shop or department store. The shaping steps for this trick are as follows:

1. Hand your dog a ring, and click and treat him for holding it.
2. Put the pole close to you and get the dog to deliver the ring close to the post; click and treat him for releasing it over the post.
3. You may help the dog by tapping the post and encouraging him to drop it. Click and treat him for gradually closer attempts to leave the ring close to the post.
4. Withhold the click and treat, and only click attempts to put the ring on the post.

With an investment of patience and time, this can be a very entertaining game for your dog to play.

Sea Hunt

For this trick, your dog has to fetch things out of a body of water. You can use a paddling pool, the bath, a bucket or a lake or pond. The target for the dog is to retrieve all the items you sink or float, and to bring them back to dry land. This is a terrific warm-weather game because it gives your dog a great way to cool off. Fill up a paddling pool with a few centimetres of water, depending on your dog's size, and sink some treasures for him to retrieve. The shaping steps for teaching your dog to play Sea Hunt are as follows:

1. Hold the object on the surface and ask the dog to Take It. Click and treat him for putting his mouth around it.
2. Hold the item just below the surface, and click and treat the dog for dipping his nose under and taking it.

3. Gradually hold the item deeper until the dog is lifting it off the bottom of the pool.
4. Vary what you get the dog to retrieve, and keep the game light and fun.
5. Vary the depth of the water as your dog gets better at this game, to make it more interesting and fun for everyone involved.

Can I throw the object I want the dog to retrieve?
The object of these exercises is to train your dog to retrieve specific, stationary objects. Throwing objects, as you would in fetch, puts your dog into prey drive, a highly charged emotional state. It is best to leave the object stationary and let him work out by your clicking which actions are rewardable and which are not.

Achoo! Can I Have a Tissue?

This trick is a real crowd-pleaser. To perform this trick, the dog has to retrieve a tissue on a sneeze cue. Who wouldn't be amazed by a dog getting you a tissue when you sneeze? For this trick, you need a pop-up box of tissues and a convincing fake sneeze. The shaping steps for teaching this trick are as follows:

1. Hand the dog a tissue, and click and treat him for taking it and holding it.
2. Take a step away, and get him to bring it to you. Click and treat him for moving towards you with the tissue in his mouth.
3. Introduce the tissue box by pulling a tissue out and laying it across the top of the box. Click and treat him for taking the tissue off the top of the box.
4. Gradually tuck the tissue in so that the dog has to pull the tissue out to get his click and treat.
5. Replace the old cue Take It with the new cue Achoo! by saying the new cue immediately before the old cue. Click and treat the dog for starting the trick as you sneeze.

Retrieving tricks are particularly impressive because they involve several steps and highlight a dog's ability to think things through to put together a great performance. Each trick involves different props, but they all involve the same basic skill of being able to pick something up and carry it back to you. Reviewing the basic retrieve with the new item is a great way to warm up any new trick, regardless of how experienced your dog may be.

Teach your dog to take a tissue without tearing it into a million pieces by giving him lots of opportunities to practise, and by not letting him hold the tissue for too long. You may also want to keep the tissue box in one place so the dog knows where to go to get a tissue when you sneeze.

CHAPTER 8

Showing-Off Tricks

We all have a little show-off in us, and dogs are no exception. Dogs love to make us laugh, and their antics often cheer us and relieve the stresses of everyday life. Taking the time to work with your dog will strengthen your bond with him and fine-tune your ability to communicate with each other. Your dog will love strutting his stuff.

Fancy Dogs

Some dogs, because of their breeds or their personalities, just seem to be suited to elegant tricks. That's why it's so important to know your dog and understand him – so you can train him to his best advantage.

Show Me Your Best Side

When your dog is performing this trick, he looks as though he is posing for a picture. This trick requires your dog to turn his head to the side and hold it. The easiest way to teach this trick is by free shaping, which means limiting the dog's options and catching the appropriate actions with a click and treat to shape the dog into the actual position that you are looking for.

1. Get with your dog to face you in a Sit, and click and treat him for staying.
2. After about 30 seconds or so, stop clicking and watch him closely; if he turns his head at all, click and treat.
3. Pick one side or the other to start with, and click any head turns in that direction.
4. When your dog starts to understand that turning his head is causing the click, it's time to delay the click by a few seconds to encourage him to hold the position.
5. Gradually increase the seconds by a few at a time until your dog will turn his head to the side and hold it for 15 seconds.
6. Name the command Pose just before he offers the turn of his head. Repeat until the command Pose causes the action.

Push a Pram

This trick is adorable, but for safety's sake it should not be practised with a real baby. A doll pram with a baby doll in it is safer. This trick requires the dog to stand and walk on his hind legs while pushing the pram with his front feet. The shaping steps for teaching Push a Pram are as follows.

1. Start by getting your dog to sniff the pram, and click and treat when he does so.
2. Secure the pram so that it won't roll, and use a target to get your dog to put his front paws on the handle; click and treat.
3. Get your dog to hold the position by delaying the click and treat by a second or two.
4. Fix the pram so that it will roll only a short distance (use blocks of wood behind the wheels), and click and treat your dog for moving the pram a little at a time.
5. Encourage your dog to move the pram, and click and treat him for doing this.
6. Control how far the pram rolls to avoid scaring your dog.
7. You can name this trick Push by saying this cue as the dog is moving the pram.

To prevent the pram from tipping over, weigh down the seat with some heavy books so that when your dog jumps up to touch the handle the pram stays stable and stationary. Make sure the wheels are locked, or use wood blocks to prevent the pram from rolling away too soon.

Hi-Ho Silver, Away!

This trick, inspired by a horse-loving friend of mine, is a great way to show off a dog that likes to jump up on you. The only difference is that your dog is not making physical contact with you when he is holding the rearing-horse position with his front legs stretched up. The shaping steps for teaching Hi-Ho Silver, Away! are as follows:

1. Hold your hand as a target above your dog's head, and click and treat him for touching it.
2. Gradually raise your hand until he is all the way up on his hind legs.
3. Practise frequently to help him build up his leg muscles.

4. Get your dog to hold the position by delaying the click and treat for several seconds.
5. Increase the time by a few seconds until he can hold the position for about 15 seconds.
6. Get your dog to extend his paws by using the Paw It command with your hand as a target.
7. Only click and treat versions of this action that are of longer duration and the right position (front paws extended).
8. Decrease the hand target by using it to start the trick and then pulling it away. Click and treat your dog for continuing to perform the action in the absence of the target.
9. Replace the old command with the new one Away by saying the new command immediately before the dog starts the trick.

Sit Up Pretty

For this trick, the dog sits on his hind legs with his front paws tucked into his chest. This is also a trick that the dog needs to practise frequently to be able to build up his back and hind-end muscles. The shaping steps for teaching Sit Up Pretty are as follows:

1. Use your hand as a target and click and treat him for touching your hand while raising his front end off the ground.
2. Withhold the click and treat by a few seconds to get your dog to hold the position high enough to have him sitting up on his rear end, but not standing.
3. Add a command such as Sit Up or Beg, saying it before the Touch one.
4. The click and treat should happen as soon as the dog starts the trick on the new command.

Practise reducing your hand as a target by presenting it but clicking before your dog actually touches it. By clicking your dog early so that he is on his way to touching your hand but doesn't actually make contact with it, he will be less dependent on its presence, and it will be easier to reduce it.

Balance a Biscuit on Your Nose

This trick demonstrates your dog's will power, because he must balance a biscuit on his nose and wait to take it until you say so.

1. Start with your dog in a Sit in front of you, and click and treat him for staying.
2. Practise holding his muzzle and placing a biscuit on his nose for a click and treat.
3. Repeat this last step until the dog can hold still for several seconds.
4. Slowly let go of your dog's muzzle and click and treat him for holding it steady.
5. Gradually increase the amount of time your dog balances the biscuit on his nose before you click and treat.
6. You will probably find after a bit of practice that your dog develops a flip-and-catch technique to eat the biscuit. This makes the trick all the more flashy and impressive.

Humble Dogs

Although some dogs are prone to fancier tricks, others are, by nature, more sedate. These simple and adorable tricks suit their personalities, and will therefore be easier for you to teach. How you use the tricks, such as Say You're Sorry, is entirely up to you.

Say You're Sorry

For this trick, the dog lies down with his chin on the ground between his front paws. An added bonus is teaching him to look up at you, which will add an even more convincing element to the performance.

1. Put your dog in a Down, facing you; click and treat him for holding that position.
2. After about 30 seconds, withhold the click and wait. Pay close attention, and click and treat any head motion down.

German
Shepherd
saying he's
sorry

3. Once your dog starts to understand that lowering his head is what causes the click, withhold the click until your dog holds the position for an extra second.
4. Increase the number of seconds your dog has to keep his head down until you can build it up to 15–20 seconds.
5. Name the action Sorry by saying the command immediately before he performs the action.
6. Repeat this step until the command Sorry starts the trick.

To help your dog understand that lowering his head is what is causing the click, deliver the treat low to encourage the dog to look down. This will give you more opportunities to reward him for doing the right action.

Say Your Prayers

Whether they are praying for leniency after getting into rubbish or praying for mud to roll in, any dog looks sweet performing this trick. This trick requires your dog to rest his paws on a chair or stool and tuck his head between his front paws. He can be either sitting or standing when he does this.

1. Use a table, stool or chair that won't move when your dog puts his paws on it.
2. Get your dog to put his front paws on the stool by tapping the stool or luring him with a treat. Click any effort to get his paws up on the stool.
3. Delay the click so that your dog is putting his paws up and leaving them there for three seconds before you click and treat.
4. Using a yogurt lid as a target, get your dog to put his head between his front paws by placing the target slightly under his chest. Click and treat your dog for making attempts to touch the target.
5. Delay the click again until your dog holds his nose to the target for longer periods of time.
6. Reduce the target slowly by clicking before he actually touches it, or by making it smaller.
7. Name the action Say Your Prayers as he is performing the trick and just before any other cues. Gradually reduce any old cues.

To make the trick Say Your Prayers go more smoothly, and to prevent your dog from scaring himself, choose a low stool that he can put his paws up on easily but that won't slide across the floor when he leans on it. Consider doing this trick on a rug or putting non-skid material under the legs of the stool.

Family Tricks

As your dog's handler, you are his connection to the human world. If your dog is part of a larger family, however, each member of the family needs to have a good working relationship with your dog. Start training your dog as an active participant in family life – everyone will benefit from it.

Wake Up Dad

What better way to wake up each morning than with a canine alarm clock? This trick requires a kiss or a nudge to the person the dog is waking up. You'll need a helper to act as the person the dog is supposed to be waking.

1. Start with the helper lying face down with his head on his folded arms. Get your helper to hide a handful of lures under his arm and encourage your dog to investigate. When your dog goes to stick his nose under the helper's arm, click and treat.
2. Decrease the lures in the helper's hand until the dog is nudging the person without the food being present. Click and treat any attempt to burrow under the person's arm.
3. Name the action Wake Up and the person's name just before the dog burrows under their arm.
4. Send your dog from gradually increasing distances until he is eagerly performing Wake Up from a room or two away.
5. Change helpers so that each member of the family gets a turn to be woken by the dog.
6. Practise every Saturday morning to make sure that no one misses out on breakfast!

As your dog begins to understand the concept of going and waking someone up, you can start to teach him to wake up specific people by getting the person to call him after you give the Wake Up command. You can wean your dog off this later when he begins to catch on.

Get Mum

This is a useful trick for kids and parents alike; for this trick, the dog must go to a family member and lead them back to the person that sent them. What better way to round up the family for dinner time then to send the dog to bring each member to the table?

1. Using the person your dog is going to get as your helper, call the dog back and forth between you, and click and treat him for going to each person.
2. When your dog is doing this enthusiastically, call the action Go and the person's name immediately before the person calls the dog to Come.
3. Gradually move the people further apart so that the dog is going to the person from different rooms and up and down the stairs.
4. Replace the Come command with Get by saying Get Mum just before Mum calls the dog to come. The person the dog is searching for should be doing the clicking and treating whenever the dog finds them.
5. Once the dog starts to perform the action each time, he can be weaned off the clicker and treats, but he should be rewarded with praise and affection.

Supersmart Tricks

You learned earlier that dogs can be trained to perform any task that they are physically capable of doing. That said, the critical factor to successfully performing these tricks is your patience in handling your dog. Using your tools (see Chapter 4) and training methods (see Chapter 7), start training your dog for these actions when you see that he is ready.

Ring a Bell

This trick involves teaching your dog to ring a bell with his nose or a paw. This trick is also quite practical, as you can teach your dog to ring a bell when he wants to go outside to relieve himself.

Hang a set of bells next to the door that you normally use to let your dog outside. Once he learns how to ring the bell with his mouth or nose, start getting him to do this each time he goes out to relieve himself. Pretty soon your dog will ring the bell to let you know he wants to go out. You may want to use a set of sleigh bells for this trick; four or five bells on a long strap may make it easier for your dog to learn to ring a bell, because it will give him more opportunities to be right.

The shaping steps for teaching your dog to Ring a Bell are as follows:

1. Put the bells on the floor and click and treat your dog for sniffing them (you can use a Touch command if he knows one).
2. Delay the click and wait for him to touch harder or mouth them before you click and treat.
3. Work at this until he's ringing the bells with purpose.
4. Hang the bells next to the door and repeat the above steps until he is ringing them regularly.
5. Gradually increase the distance he must travel to touch the bells.
6. Verbally name ringing the bells, Bells.

Dancing Dog

This trick is adorable but difficult for most dogs. To perform this trick, the dog must balance on his hind legs and walk. You'll want to practise this in short sessions to help your dog build up his back and leg muscles gradually. Be sure to work on a non-skid surface so that your dog does not injure himself, and stop immediately if the dog appears to be in pain. The shaping steps for teaching Dancing Dog are as follows:

1. With your dog in a Sit, hold your hand slightly above his nose, and click and treat any effort to raise himself up on his back legs to touch your hand.
2. Raise your hand higher, and continue to click and treat your dog for using his hind end to raise himself up and touch your hand.
3. Get your dog to hold the position longer by delaying the click by a second or two.
4. Gradually increase the time to several seconds.
5. Move your hand around, and click and treat him for walking on his hind legs to touch it.
6. Turn your hand in a circle, and click and treat your dog for walking on his hind legs to follow it.
7. Add the command Dance by saying it just before the dog starts to perform the trick.

Get Me a Bottle of Water

This amazing trick involves your dog opening the fridge, taking out a bottle of water, closing the door and bringing the bottle of water to you. You'll probably want to start with a water bottle and then, as your dog refines his techniques, you can change the water bottle to a tin or a bottle of juice. This trick has three different parts: retrieving the bottle, opening the fridge door, and closing the fridge door.

Getting the Water Bottle

1. Hand your dog a bottle of water and tell him to Take It. Click and treat your dog for hanging on to it for several seconds at a time.
2. Move away from your dog and get him to come to you over greater and greater distances. Click and treat him first as he is moving to you, and then for delivering the bottle to your hand.
3. Place the bottle on the floor and tell your dog to Take It then Bring It. Click and treat him for retrieving it, then gradually withhold the click until the dog is on his way back to you.
4. Put the bottle on a low shelf of the fridge and practise getting the dog to Take It. Click and treat your dog for at first approaching, then taking then bringing the bottle to you over short training sessions.

Golden Retriever with baby bottle

Opening the Fridge Door

1. Put a strap on the fridge door to make it easier for your dog to open it.
2. Starting with the fridge door open, hand your dog the strap and tell him Take It. Click and treat him for taking the strap.
3. Once your dog is taking the strap regularly, delay the click for an extra second or two and click and treat your dog for holding it.
4. Standing slightly behind your dog, call him back to you while he holds the strap. You may need to go back and teach your dog the formal retrieve (see Chapter 7) with the strap, or at least review it with him.
5. When he can hold onto the strap while backing away, click and treat him for actually moving the door.
6. Gradually close the door until it's almost clicked shut, so that your dog has to pull harder to open it.
7. Once your dog can open it when it's shut all the way, try letting him retrieve the strap on his own. At first, click and treat any attempt to take the strap.
8. Gradually add a little distance so that your dog is approaching the fridge from greater and greater distances.
9. Eventually delay your click so that your dog is taking the strap and starting to back away to pull the door open before you click. If at any time he seems confused and the trick falls apart, go back and break things down into smaller parts and gradually rebuild the trick.

Close the Door (dog uses his nose)

1. Once your dog is comfortable holding the bottle in his mouth, practise having him target the fridge door with his nose.
2. Open the door a little, give a Touch command, and click and treat him for moving the door shut even a little.
3. Gradually leave the door open a little more, until the dog is shutting the door with purpose. Make sure you click and treat your dog for even small attempts to push the door shut.
4. Verbally name the command Shut the Door.

Close the Door (dog uses his paws)

An alternative option would be to have your dog use his paws on the fridge to close it (see Chapter 4).

1. Use a paw target to get him to touch the fridge with his paws, then click and treat.
2. Open the door a little and tell your dog to paw the door; click and treat him for pushing the door shut.
3. Gradually open the door more so your dog has to push the door harder to earn the click and treat.
4. Verbally name the command Shut the Door.

Be careful what item you choose for your dog to retrieve. Water bottles are the easiest for the dog to grasp at first, and later you can work up to retrieving tins or bottles. If you have a dog that tends to bite down hard when he retrieves things, you may want to practise with empty tins first to prevent him from scaring himself or making a mess of your kitchen.

Review each piece to put them all together. Open the fridge door (keep the bottle on the lower shelf), and get your dog to take the bottle. When he still has the bottle in his mouth, call him around the door and tell him to push it shut. Practise these two steps until they are fluid. Then add the command to Take It (the door strap), followed by retrieving the bottle. Practise these together until they are fluid. Then combine them with closing the door. You may have to go back and forth a bit in order to keep each separate part of the trick strong until eventually it is one continuous action.

Go Left, Go Right

Teaching your dog how to distinguish between his left and right will amaze your friends and family. It will also enable you to direct your dog to exactly where you want him to go.

1. Start with your dog in front of an object (such as a chair or a footstool), and put a target lid to the left about 1m (3ft) away.
2. Send your dog to Touch, and click and treat him for responding.
3. Repeat this at gradually increasing distances, clicking right before your dog touches his nose to the target.
4. When your dog is performing the action easily, say the new cue Go Left just before he is about to move forwards to touch the target. Repeat this until he will go to the left when you say left.
5. Reduce the target by making it smaller (use scissors to cut it into smaller pieces) until your dog simply moves left on command.
6. To teach your dog Go Right, simply follow all the same steps except with everything on the right.

You can combine the Go Left and Go Right commands with retrieving tricks by lining up several objects in a row and asking your dog to take the one on the left or the right. If nothing else, this trick will give you a better foundation for teaching your dog more complicated tricks.

Find It

Sending your dog to find something you have lost is useful for you and exciting for the dog. Losing a wallet or keys in a pile of leaves or along your walking route could be disastrous – unless your dog can help in the search.

1. Choose an item with lots of your scent on it (such as a hat or a hair band) and show it to your dog.
2. Get someone to hold your dog's collar while you hide the item somewhere obvious at first.
3. Release your dog to go and find it, and click and treat him as he approaches it.
4. Gradually increase the difficulty by hiding the object in ever more challenging places.
5. Find another item to practise with, and try again.
6. Name the action Find It as the dog moves towards the object.

Multi-Dog Tricks

Successful multi-dog tricks can only work when each dog understands the action and can perform it on a reliable cue. Before attempting it with more than one dog, go over the steps with each dog individually. If things fall apart or don't go as well as planned, review the steps with each dog separately.

These tricks are meant to be performed by two or three dogs at once. You may want to enlist the help of multiple handlers, one for each dog. The helpers' roles will be to reinforce and reward individual dogs for performing correctly while they get used to performing tricks as a team.

Double-Dog Roll Over

This trick involves two dogs rolling over at the same time. As you position the dogs, make sure that you leave enough space in between them so that they don't crash into each other. Another way you could perform this trick would be to have the dogs roll over one at a time, one right after the other. Shaping steps for the Double-Dog Roll Over are as follows:

1. Get each dog to lie about 1m (3ft) apart (allow more space if the dogs are giant breeds).
2. Praise each dog for holding the Down/Stay position.
3. Command the dogs to Roll Over one at a time (praise the others for staying until they have been called), or give the command for all the dogs to roll at the same time.
4. Experiment with giving a command to each dog and then giving one to the group, and see which version of the trick looks better.
5. If you are commanding all the dogs at once, you need only one click for all of them, but reward each dog with his own treat.
6. If you are commanding each dog separately, click and treat that dog before asking the next one to go.

7. Once the dogs are performing reliably, go ahead and verbally name the trick Everybody Over, or name each individual roll over with the dog's name and then the Roll Over command.

Pass the Biscuit, Please

This trick requires two dogs, one sitting in front of the other. The first dog balances a biscuit on his nose, and on command tosses his head back, flinging the biscuit over his head to the dog sitting behind him. The dog sitting behind him catches it and eats it as his reward.

Shaping steps for teaching the first dog to balance a biscuit on his nose are as follows:

1. Choose a flat biscuit to help the dog learn to balance it.
2. Hold your dog's muzzle still, and click and treat him for allowing you to do this.
3. Place a dog biscuit on the flat part of the top of his muzzle, and click and treat him for holding his head still.
4. Use a Stay command and frequent clicks and treats to help your dog learn to balance the biscuit on his nose.
5. Once he's got the balancing part, you can click after a certain number of seconds and release him to flip the biscuit off his nose.

It requires good timing of the click to get your dog to understand that it's the toss of his head that you are looking for. Most dogs will toss their heads back to get the biscuit off their nose. Some will even flip it and catch it if you practise enough. It's important that you let your dog develop his own style by practising frequently.

Add the second dog to the mix once your biscuit-balancing dog has a good toss and is no longer immediately pursuing the dropped biscuit. Practise getting the second dog to catch the biscuit after the first dog tosses it. This may require lots of practice to get the timing and coordination just right. The commands or names will be Hold It, Stay and then OK, which will cause the dog holding the biscuit to toss it; this will be caught by the dog behind him. Make sure you click and treat the first dog for not pursuing the tossed biscuit.

When getting a group of dogs to perform together, you might like to stagger the actions so that the dogs perform them one after the other. Initially, you may want to use a helper to reinforce the dogs that are waiting for their turn.

Everybody Wave

This adorable trick can be performed with any number of dogs. The dogs should line up facing their audience and raise a paw in the air as if waving hello. The shaping steps for teaching a group of dogs to wave are as follows:

1. Make sure each dog can fluently and reliably wave on a hand signal.
2. Line the dogs up and praise them for holding a Stay.
3. Command the dogs to Wave, and click and treat all of them.
4. Practise with two dogs at a time until they are competing with each other to raise their paws the fastest.
5. Encourage extra-fast efforts by clicking and treating only the dog that was first.
6. Gradually add more dogs, following the same rules; the faster dogs get treated more often than the slower dogs.
7. If one dog is particularly slow, take him aside and teach him to wave faster before putting him back into the group.

This trick is an adorable way to say hello or goodbye during a visit to schoolchildren or to a nursing home. You can vary how you have the dogs perform it by getting them to wave individually or as a group. You can also improve on each dog's individual wave by only clicking and treating the best versions of the wave, one aspect at a time. For instance, you might improve the speed of the dog's response by giving the cue and only clicking and treating when he performs the action within a certain amount of time (say three seconds). You might improve the height of the wave by only clicking and treating the higher waves and ignoring the lower ones, telling the dog to try again. Just be sure that you are concentrating on one aspect at a time, so as not to confuse the dog.

Leapfrog

Be careful which dogs you choose for this trick; not all dogs are comfortable letting other dogs jump over them. This trick requires two to three dogs. While the rest of the dogs lie down about 1m (3ft) apart, the third dog leaps over their backs and lies down next to the last dog. The first dog then repeats this, and so on.

1. Praise all the dogs for lying down and holding the Stay.
2. Work the first dog by getting him to touch his nose to the target stick held over the back of the first dog. Use the target stick to help him hop over the other dogs one at a time; click and treat each hop.
3. When the last dog has been hopped over, get him to lie down and let the next dog go.
4. Praise the other dogs for holding the Down/Stay position. You may need a helper for this.
5. To increase your dog's tolerance for being hopped over, practise praising your dog for letting other dogs step over him.
6. Adding speed to this trick will make it impressive; just be sure to build up to it slowly, and don't rush the dogs – when they are comfortable, they will move faster.

Evaluate the dogs that you use for this trick carefully, and make sure that they don't mind having a dog jump over their back. This is not a trick that every dog will tolerate.

Take a Bow

For this trick, the dog brings his front end close to the ground, with his chest resting on the floor, lifts his tail end in the air and holds the position. You can get the dogs to do it all at the same time, or one after the other.

1. It's probably best to start with all the dogs in the Sit/Stay position. Praise each dog for holding the Stay.
2. Give the command Bow to all the dogs at once or each dog individually. Click and treat those dogs that do the action correctly.
3. Continue to practise until all the dogs are performing in unison. Don't be afraid to go back and review the steps with each dog individually if the trick starts to fall apart. (See Chapter 6 for the shaping steps for teaching your dog to bow.)

If you are going to train multiple dogs to work together, it's a good idea to make sure they get along well and are not competitive over food. Each dog should be taught how to perform the trick separately until the trick is on a reliable command before being asked to perform it in a group. If you do not have the trick reliably on call with the dogs individually, a group training session will be a frustrating experience for all of you.

Walking the Dog

This trick involves two dogs. One dog wears a collar and lead, and the other dog carries the lead in his mouth.

1. Teach your dog to retrieve and carry a lead. (See Chapter 7 for shaping the retrieve action.)
2. Once your dog is retrieving the lead easily, start practising getting him to hold it with some resistance (hold onto the end and give a little tug).
3. Hand your dog the lead, and click and treat him for taking it and walking with you.
4. With the lead firmly in your dog's mouth, practise giving it a tug, and click and treat him for pulling back or hanging on.
5. Gradually increase the amount of resistance you offer, to prepare him for a real dog on the end of the lead.
6. When he can carry the lead while you are offering resistance, go ahead and add a real dog.

7. The dog you add should be an adult with some lead training, and the lead should be attached to a flat buckled collar.
8. The dog being led should be clicked and treated for walking slightly ahead of the other dog but not pulling.

Tips for a Better Performance

When working with multiple dogs, it quickly becomes apparent that the better able the dogs are to perform the tricks alone, the more likely they are to cooperate as a group. There are some tricks to working with groups of dogs that understand what is expected but need to learn how to do the trick in unison.

· Only treat those dogs that perform the trick quickly.
· Point to the individual dog you are working with as you command.
· Use a helper to reward the other dogs for holding a Stay while you work with an individual dog.
· Review tricks regularly with each individual dog to keep the whole performance consistent.
· Vary the quality and quantity of treats to keep your dog guessing and trying harder to earn the next treat.
· Keep your sessions short and frequent to keep the dogs focused and sharp.

It can't be stressed enough that if you don't reward the dogs that are awaiting their turn to perform, you will lose their interest. Rewarding the dogs that are waiting will ensure that all the dogs stay focused and ready to work.

The show-off in every dog is something to celebrate! Let your dog – or dogs – indulge his sense of humour and excitement by making him part of your entertainment committee. Enjoy spending time teaching your dog tricks and performing them for friends and family. Developing a healthy training relationship with your dog will make it easier to communicate with him and help you to gain control of behaviour problems.

CHAPTER 9

Techniques and Tools for Problem-Solving

I f you don't train your dog or provide any structure, you will be rewarded with a dog that behaves exactly as you taught him to behave: in ways that are out of control, demanding, mischievous and destructive. Invest the time, patience and love to get your dog off to a good start, and you will have a companion that enhances your and your family's life.

Set the Best Environment

Living with a dog need not be complicated, but with the changing demands of life in our world, dogs are left to cope with an amazing amount of stress and changes that their ancestors never had to

deal with. To say that our schedules are going to change dramatically when we take on a dog as a member of our family is unrealistic; however, we must make accommodations for dogs and be sure we meet their needs. If we are unable or unwilling to spend more time at home with our pets, we must be willing to hire someone to take care of their needs for us.

Dogs are pack animals that were meant to live in groups; they are not solitary animals and do not enjoy spending hours alone for days at a time. The root of many dogs' behaviour problems lies in a lack of stimulation and energy outlets. Most people can't just leave their jobs to stay at home with the dog, but the emergence of quality day kennels and reputable pet sitters has made it possible to own a dog and have a busy life.

Who will exercise your dog if you can't?
For many dogs, having a dog walker to play with in the middle of the day, or spending a day at a reputable kennel, is not a frivolous luxury; it's necessary exercise and social time with other dogs and people.

Behaviour problems in dogs lead many people to seek help from a dog trainer or attend a group training class. Problems usually range from jumping or mouthing to excessive barking or aggression. If you visit an animal shelter, you will see many dogs between the age of nine months and two years, whose families simply didn't have time for their energy and antics. Behaviour problems don't have to lead to the dog being left at an animal shelter if you understand a little about how dogs think and what motivates them to do what they do.

When you take a dog into your home, you must make room for him. Dogs require a lot of love and training and care, but they give so much more back in loyalty and love. Be sure to give him the best home you possibly can – you will be rewarded a hundredfold. If your dog's behaviour is less than ideal, don't give up. All dogs, no matter how sweet and compliant they are, need training, limits, exercise and house rules.

Analyze the Problem

When it comes to trying to solve a dog's behaviour problem, people often think too much. They blame the dog for soiling the carpet out of spite, when in reality the dog isn't being walked enough! Let's be clear here: dogs don't hold grudges, they don't do things out of spite and they are not sorry for anything! Dogs are not capable of those thoughts. They live in the moment, they are opportunistic and they repeat behaviour that is rewarded, even if it's rewarded negatively. That's why we like dogs, remember? They are not little people in fur suits; they are dogs.

Dogs are animals, and animals do things that sometimes baffle humans, despite our best attempts to understand them. In order to solve an existing behaviour problem, it is crucial to sit down with your family members and figure out the details of the problem. Using the following questions as a guide, try to identify and define what the dog is actually doing, when he is doing it, and what you might be able to teach him to do instead.

Identify the problem. What does the dog actually do? Write it down and describe it in as much detail as possible.
Cause. What triggers the dog to act in this way? Is it the presence of a strange dog, the doorbell or a new person?

Frequency. How often does the dog do what he does? Once a minute, non-stop, every time the trigger is present, only half the time?

Consequence. What has been done to stop the dog? What consequence results when the dog responds to the trigger?

Reinforcement history. How long has the dog been acting in this manner, and what is causing him to repeat it?

Management. What can you do to prevent the dog from repeating the behaviour while you are retraining him?

By identifying the actual source of the problem, you will be able to develop a plan for retraining the dog to respond in a more appropriate way. Let everyone who takes care of the dog participate in the exercise, as well as in future training sessions.

Managing Behaviour

Prevention isn't training, but it can help you get rid of unwanted behaviour, because you are not allowing the dog to practise it repeatedly. 'Managing' involves putting the dog in a separate room or crate when visitors come, or stepping on the lead to prevent the dog from jumping. The less the dog gets to do the wrong behaviour, the less you will have to do to convince him that the right behaviour is more rewarding and desirable. Managing behaviour does *not* mean correcting, reprimanding or punishing your dog.

Some people manage their dog's behaviour with crates, gates and pens; others use leads or going out. It doesn't matter how you manage your dog's behaviour, as long as it keeps your dog from doing the wrong things over and over again. You want to change problem behaviour, and management prevents the dog from rewarding himself. Consider these behaviour-management ideas:

· Use a crate when you can't watch your dog, particularly if he is a destructive chewer.

· Keep a lead on your dog when people come to visit, and put your foot on it to prevent jumping.

· Don't allow your dog off the lead in public places if he doesn't come when he's called.
· Avoid other dogs if your dog is aggressive around them.
· If your dog likes to escape out of the front door, deny access to it.
· If your dog likes to bite the postman, don't tie him outside the front door.
· If your dog is not fully housetrained yet, don't allow him unsupervised freedom.

Management and prevention are things you can do to keep a behaviour problem from perpetuating itself; use them while you are retraining your dog to do something more appropriate. Prevention is not a 100 per cent solution, but it can help you move towards your target by not reinforcing any inappropriate behaviour.

Alternative Behaviour

Okay. You've got to the root of the bad behaviour, and you have an interim plan in place – management. The next step is understanding reinforcement and replacement behaviour. You need to provide reinforcement for behaviour other than what you don't like. Otherwise, the dog will revert to the old behaviour. Think about praising a habit that is easy to teach and easy for the dog to perform, even when there are a lot of distractions.

Most dog owners know exactly what they want their dogs to stop doing, but very few have put thought into what the dog should do instead. Unless you develop a plan for an acceptable alternative, you will not get rid of problem behaviour.

What Causes Wrong Behaviour?

Look closely at the circumstances surrounding misbehaviour, and see what the dog finds pleasing about it. If he jumps and people yell at him and push him off, perhaps he likes the attention that this provides, and they should ignore him instead. Maybe there is a member of your household that encourages the dog to jump and isn't consistent about praising the dog for sitting instead.

By removing the source of the habit, you can go a long way to getting rid of a behaviour problem. In many cases, the dog is getting far too much attention for the wrong behaviour and needs more information about what is going right. If there isn't anything going right, then the dog has too much freedom and too many options. In this case, you'll need to rethink your training programme and make it easier for your dog to learn the correct behaviour.

Encouraging the Correct Behaviour

To change behaviour that has become a habit, you need to provide a high rate of encouragement and praise for the appropriate behaviour, or it will never occur to the dog to try anything else. Dogs do what works, so if they get attention for the wrong behaviour, they are likely to repeat it in the future. If they are encouraged for more appropriate behaviour with really tasty treats or exciting games of fetch, they will tend to make the good things happen again by repeating the behaviour.

Providing an undesirable consequence for a bad habit, such as turning away from a barking dog, is very effective in changing the habit. Being ignored was not the outcome the dog expected; by ignoring him, you are saying that barking doesn't work.

Every encouragement for the correct behaviour is like money in the bank. If your dog's bank account for the undesirable behaviour is high, you will need to build up a considerable history of encouragement and reward for the alternate behaviour. Practise often, give occasional jackpots (a handful of small goodies or an extra-long game of fetch or tug), and get your dog prepared to succeed.

Training Incompatible Behaviour

Teaching the dog what is acceptable behaviour solves many behaviour problems because a dog can't necessarily do two things at once. For instance, a dog can't sit politely to greet a stranger and jump on them at the same time. Giving the dog an alternative reaction gives you more control over him, and it also allows you to reward him for an appropriate response. Perhaps your dog could:

- Greet visitors with a toy in his mouth instead of jumping on them.
- Go to his bed or mat when the doorbell rings.
- Do a play bow when he sees another dog.
- Retrieve a toy instead of barking at the window at passers-by.
- Look at you instead of lunging at other dogs.
- Target your hand (see Chapter 4) instead of running away.

Use this opportunity to be creative and find solutions that suit your needs and your dog's natural inclinations. Think of this as another way you're making it easy for training to be successful.

Problem-Solving Tools

Every dog owner needs to be armed with tools and tricks to teach their dog how to live with people in a safe, relaxed manner. Knowing your dog well – his energy level, his tolerance of other dogs, his likes and dislikes – will be a huge asset in training him to respond to you in appropriate ways.

The most reliable outcome of punishment is a breakdown of the relationship and the trust that we have worked so hard to cultivate. Punishment doesn't change behaviour permanently unless there is an incentive to do something else.

Map out the changes to your dog's routine that you have decided to implement, and determine a time frame for training him. Set up a schedule of consistent practice times so that you teach each part of each trick in small digestible portions, to be built upon each time you work your dog. Make sure you also consider the whole dog, mind and body, and provide for all your dog's needs.

Exercise

Don't let this become ignored or neglected. Playing, running, fetching and having time with you is crucial to a dog's sanity. Be sure that your dog gets at least 30–60 minutes a day of all-out running or playtime with other dogs before you even consider training him to be a better companion. If your dog has tons of toys but only plays with a few, consider grouping them in sets of ten and rotating them each week to keep things interesting. Make a play date with your neighbour's dog, sign up for a day care kennel, or hire a pet sitter to exercise your dog while you're at work so that when you come home you can concentrate on training your dog and have a willing student who is ready to work.

Basic Obedience

Nothing beats the companionship of a well-trained dog. A dog that responds to Sit, Down and Come is a dog that can be taken to many places and not put you to shame. Spend time teaching these basics, at first in an environment with only a few distractions, and then build up to being able to work somewhere out of doors or around other dogs.

Teaching your dog to Sit, Lie Down and Come is useful and can replace unwanted behaviour. In order for your dog's training to be effective, you must practise often, and the dog's response to commands must not be dependent on the environment or the presence of food. Weaning your dog off food lures and lots of extra commands and prompting will make you both relaxed in public, because you will know just what to expect from each other.

If your dog's response to commands around distractions falls apart, it simply means you have more training to do. Manipulating the variables slowly in order to maintain your dog's response to commands is one key to success. If you work at it, it won't be long before you are rewarded with an obedient dog that you can take anywhere.

Consider taking a group class. The distraction of other dogs will help your dog realize that he must learn to pay attention to you. At the class, try to make sure the ratio of teacher to student is high; 12 students to two instructors is ideal.

Self-Control Exercises

Dogs don't learn self-control unless they are allowed to make choices and are rewarded for making good ones. Using a clicker and treats to mark and reward behaviour is critical. The clicker allows you to mark the right choice and begin a savings account for the appropriate actions and behaviour. The following exercise, Choose to Sit, is one example of helping your dog learn self-control.

1. Greet visitors with the dog on a lead.
2. If the dog jumps, the visitor goes away.
3. If the dog sits, the visitor stays and the handler clicks and treats.
4. The dog learns by trial and error how to get the person to pay attention to him.
5. The handler supplies information by clicking and treating the correct responses.
6. The visitor supplies consequences for not sitting by not allowing the dog to say hello to her.

As you try to solve your dog's behaviour problems, keep this example in mind. Learning will last longer when the dog works out on his own what the rewardable behaviour is, especially if the dog is usually excellent when there are no distractions, but falls apart in public.

Golden
Retriever
weaving
through legs

The next exercise is another self-control exercise that helps your dog work out how to pay attention to you. The Attention Game is intended to teach your dog to look at you frequently and to ignore distractions. In time, teaching your dog to look at you will give him a greater awareness of you, which will improve his recall and heeling commands. Dogs who have some responsibility to know where you are will not stray far away when they are off their lead. They will check you regularly and come back easily when you call, because they know you are in control. Here's how the game works:

1. In a quiet room, sit in a chair with your dog on a lead.
2. Ignore your dog until he looks in your direction, then click and treat.
3. Ignore him again until he looks back at you, then click and treat.

4. Time yourself for one minute and count how many times he looks at you in that minute. If your dog looks at you six or more times in one minute, you are ready to add distractions.
5. Do this again in a new place or with a distraction, and repeat the one-minute test. The distraction is too intense if your dog looks at you less than twice a minute.
6. Repeat this until your dog is looking at you six or more times a minute, and then change the distraction again.
7. If your dog doesn't look at you more than twice in a minute for several repetitions, you will probably need to move away from the distraction or go somewhere less distracting.
8. Increase the quality and quantity of the rewards every once in a while, to intensify the dog's response and to increase the likelihood that he will look at you more often.
9. Reward exceptional behaviour. If your dog ignores an unexpected distraction, be sure to reward him with a whole handful of goodies to reinforce the good performance.

Your aim with this game is to increase your dog's attention to you. As a result of paying attention to you, your dog is learning to block out distractions and maintain self-control.

Having techniques and tools to help you teach your dog what is expected of him will not only make your training sessions run smoothly, it will make solving behaviour problems that much more productive. Behaviour problems need not be mysterious or result in your surrendering of your dog to already overflowing animal shelters. With a little knowledge and skill, you can teach your dog to be a well-behaved member of your family.

CHAPTER 10

A Word About Punishment

As humans, we are absolutely convinced that in order to change behaviour we must provide some sort of punishment that will eliminate bad behaviour altogether. But in truth, no animals, including humans, respond well to punishment. Although it has been part of training dogs for decades, punishment is not a good or effective way to develop a well-behaved family pet.

Punishment Can Make Things Worse

Over a period of time, many trainers have found that it is totally unnecessary to use punishment in order to get reliable, acceptable behaviour. In many cases, using punishment can actually make some problems worse. Consider these two points:

- Punishment stops bad behaviour, but it does not teach or provide another choice.
- The many negative side effects of punishment outweigh the short-term benefits.

The best human example of why punishment is ineffective is a speeding ticket. If you've ever been pulled over for speeding, you'll understand. The moment the lights flash behind you is horrible. When you're actually pulled over, your heart races, you stutter and stammer, and you wait and wait and wait. Now you've got a fine to pay, and penalty points on your licence as well. Do you stop driving above the speed limit? Well, for a little while you do, but one day you are late, you speed again, and this time you get away with it.

You may have been a little more careful this time, avoiding speed cameras and keeping your eyes open, but you were speeding. After being punished severely only weeks before, how could you go back to that behaviour? Quite simply, the punishment made you a better speeder! You are no longer a random, careless speeder; you actually look for police cars and avoid known speed traps. The punishment actually improved the way you speed.

Punishment Is Reactive

The first problem with punishment is that it is a response to bad behaviour, whereas training initiates good behaviour. The second problem with punishment as a training tool is that you can't always control what the student learns. In fact, punishment puts the subject in an excitable and defensive emotional state, which interferes with the dog's ability to learn anything.

Another reason that punishment is not very effective for curing behaviour problems is that it is only part of the equation. Punishment only stops the unwanted behaviour; it does not show the dog what he should have done instead. Punishment occurs too late to teach anything, because by the time it is delivered, the dog has already performed the undesirable behaviour and cannot undo it.

Management tools (Chapter 9) will result in a well-behaved dog without the fallout of a deteriorating relationship and the breakdown of trust that most punishment causes. Management eliminates the opportunity for wrong behaviour, making it easier for your dog to choose the right one.

Punishing your dog for jumping on the visitors will not make him want to sit in front of them next time. In fact, punishment delivered by a visitor or in the presence of one might actually teach your dog to be fearful of visitors, because it's sometimes unpleasant to be around them. This is not what you want to teach. After working so hard to make sure that your dog is social around people, it would be detrimental to all to start punishing him for being friendly.

Timing Is Everything

If you are going to use punishment and if it is to mean anything, the timing of the correction has to be precise; it must happen the moment the undesirable behaviour begins. Not many people, especially the average pet owner, are capable of doing this. Another issue with the timing of the correction is that the dog is probably overstimulated and excited, which means his brain is not in learning mode. In order to process information, a dog has to be in a fairly relaxed state.

If the timing of the correction were perfect, the dog would need to be rewarded as soon as the inappropriate behaviour stopped. The timing of the reward here is the instructive part for the dog. If the behaviour that we are trying to change is one the dog has been doing for a long time, a very high rate of reinforcement for the right behaviour must be employed, or the new, desirable behaviour will not replace the old behaviour. Remember that old habits die hard, and it is difficult to adopt new ways of doing things without being readily prepared for the right choices.

Once your dog is overexcited, he can't learn anything. His behaviour will either get more frantic, or he will shut down completely. The person delivering the punishment is likely to add more punishment, continuing the unproductive cycle, and no real learning happens.

Redirecting Behaviour

Rather than doing corrections (a polite word for 'punishment'), either redirect or interrupt the dog before he starts the behaviour. At the first sign of alert or tension, the dog must be interrupted and redirected to more appropriate behaviour. An interruption could be something like saying the dog's name, touching the dog on the shoulder, or turning away from whatever captured the dog's interest.

Pay attention to your dog's levels of distraction and excitement. Overstimulation will prevent him from learning anything. Build up to working around intense distractions, rather than jumping into chaos and hoping for the best.

To work effectively, interruptions must be delivered before the dog starts the behaviour. In the case of barking, for instance, if you wait until the dog is barking and frantic you will not be able to distract him from what he's barking at in order to teach him anything. For some single-minded dogs, you could use a strong correction and it still wouldn't concern him one bit, let alone stop his behaviour. It would be like trying to reason with someone who is angry – a person who is not in a rational frame of mind is not capable of listening to you or being reasonable.

Golden Retriever holding the telephone

Instead, start paying attention to what triggers the barking, and interrupt the dog while he's still thinking about it. To short-circuit undesirable behaviour, you might get the dog to go to his bed, or move further away from the distractions so he's not as excited. Your aim is to interrupt him close to the distractions in the environments where he performs the undesirable behaviour, but it is unreasonable to try to train him there in the beginning. As with any constructive and lasting training, you need to start with small, simple steps that enable the dog to be successful.

As you work out a plan for what you want your dog to do, it's important to write it out and continue to act on it. Make sure any treats, a clicker or other equipment are conveniently located in your house or garden, allowing you to reward your dog whenever the opportunity arises. If the new behaviour is complicated, break it down into steps and practise with your dog frequently. Make sure you keep everything simple.

Establishing New Patterns

In order to stop unwanted behaviour and get your dog to develop new patterns, you need to have a set plan to accomplish your aim, and you must also prevent the dog from doing the old behaviour while you are retraining him. Setting up a new pattern of behaviour isn't easy for dogs, because they get into habits, just as we do, and tend to do things the same way again and again if they can.

Repetition

The important thing to remember when changing a pattern is that you need to practise the new pattern over and over again, and reward the dog repeatedly for the new behaviour until he adopts it as his own. In the meantime, if you want to speed up where you are going, you need to stop allowing the dog to commit the wrong behaviour by preventing it from happening. For example, stepping on the dog's lead to prevent him jumping will not, in itself, teach your dog to sit, but it will reduce his options and make sitting more likely, because that is the only behaviour that is being rewarded.

An Ounce of Prevention

The more time you spend with dogs, the more you will find that a large part of training is really management. Gates, crates and pens can be your best friends when raising and training a dog. Although they don't teach the dog not to chew the couch or pee on the carpet, they prevent inappropriate behaviour from turning into bad habits. Managing a dog's environment helps him to be right by limiting his choices. It isn't the solution to all of your behaviour problems, but it is an integral part of it.

When you pay attention to what's going right and ignore what the dog is doing wrong, you'll begin to reap the rewards. Dogs are social creatures that crave attention, so even negative attention when they are misbehaving may be encouragement enough to repeat the very behaviour you are trying so hard to eliminate.

For example, a fence is a management tool for dogs that enjoy playing in their garden and owners who want to keep them there. A baby gate in the kitchen limits the dog's freedom so that he can't get into trouble in the rest of the house. When you don't have time to teach your dog to sit for a guest, putting your dog behind a gate would be a better way to manage his jumping problem than letting him dive on the person or run out of the front door.

The Fallout of Punishment: Aggression

If punishment is mistimed or too severe, it can often cause the dog to turn and bite whoever is closest. Dogs that are corrected for barking and lunging at other dogs and people don't learn to like them; in fact, many of these animals become more unpredictable and dangerous. They learn that the presence of other dogs or people means they are about to get punished, so they will often bite without warning.

Warnings Work for a Reason

If you physically punish a dog for growling, he may stop growling and go straight to the bite instead. You have made that dog far more dangerous because he no longer warns people that he is not comfortable, he just bites them. You have, in essence, created a better biter. Growling is a dog's way of warning us that he is uncomfortable and that if the person or dog doesn't go away there's going to be trouble. Punishing the warning doesn't make sense; we want to change the way the dog feels about the person or dog, not take away the warning that he is about to bite. This is nature's way of letting us know we have a problem and gives us time to do something about it (such as teaching the dog a positive association with people and dogs) before the dog bites.

Training Versus Punishment

Never use punishment with any problem related to aggression around people or dogs – the risk of creating an aggressive dog is just too great. Here are five reasons to teach your dog instead of punishing him.

1. Punishment must be repeated frequently to remind the dog to avoid his mistake.
2. Punishment doesn't teach the dog anything; dogs with little confidence will become more timid.
3. With punishment, you can't control what the dog learns.
4. Punishment can damage the relationship between owner and dog.
5. Punishment can accelerate aggression by suppressing all precursors to aggression so that the dog goes straight to the bite.

There are many reasons for not using punishment in training your dog to be a better companion. In general, punishment misses the point. It comes too late to be instructive, and has the danger of teaching the dog to be better at the very behaviour we are trying to eliminate.

Shetland Sheepdog targeting a plastic lid

If your dog is behaving so poorly that you think he needs punishment, then the real problem is that he needs more information about what he has to do to be right. Instead of spending your time working out how to stop the behaviour you don't like, map out what you want the dog to do instead and retrain him.

Aggression and nervousness are emotional states where the dog is in a fight-or-flight mode, not a learning mode. In this frame of mind, a dog is unable to learn anything. He must be comfortable, not defensive, in order to learn appropriate non-aggressive responses.

If a dog's basic needs for exercise, training and attention are met and he is carefully managed according to his age and training level, you will have fewer behaviour problems and fewer bad habits to correct. Think carefully about how you use punishment, because it is often an indicator of a much larger issue. If you want a well-behaved dog that responds to you quickly and is fun to be around, don't use punishment to teach him; it won't get you where you want to go.

CHAPTER 11

Training for Better Behaviour

When dealing with behaviour problems, it is essential that you plan out what your dog should do in place of the behaviour you are trying to eliminate. If you want to change inappropriate behaviour permanently, you must replace it with the correct behaviour and heavily reinforce it, or no real change will occur.

Have a Plan

Many dog owners know exactly what they don't want their dogs to do, but very few have given much thought to what the dog should do instead. Leaving your dog with too many choices may lead to your dog choosing incorrectly and you being frustrated that he's not 'getting it', which is unfair on both of you.

In order to have a dog that is trained to be responsive and enjoyable, you will need to get your family's act together. The fastest way to change your dog's unwanted behaviour is to stop reinforcing the incorrect behaviour and start reinforcing alternative behaviour in its place. There are endless possibilities to choose from. Sit down with your family and review the behaviour questions in Chapter 9. Then come up with ideas on how you want your dog to respond in different situations. When choosing which behaviour to reinforce, you'll want to keep these points in mind:

- Keep it simple.
- Choose something incompatible with the wrong behaviour.
- Plan ahead and be prepared (carry your treats and clicker with you).
- Control the variables (such as distractions and the environment).
- Avoid reinforcing the wrong behaviour.
- Build a savings account for good behaviour.
- Teach your dog to be well-behaved anywhere.

Each time the dog gets to practise old, undesirable behaviour, he is putting money in the bank for doing that action again. Preventing the wrong things from happening is half of the training.

Keep It Simple

Whatever you choose as the alternative actions should be simple for the dog to offer quickly and reliably. Choose a single command, such as Sit or Down, and reinforce it frequently. If the command is too complicated or involved, your dog may lose interest and go back to the undesirable behaviour. A simple command, such as Sit, is something you are likely to notice and reinforce even in a distracting environment. Be sure your dog knows the command well by applying the Ten in a Row rule.

Choose a Compatible Command

Make sure that the new action is quite different to the undesirable behaviour. For instance, a dog cannot sit and jump at the same time. If you reinforce sitting as the desirable action when your dog greets new people, it won't be long before your dog doesn't even try to jump. Be forewarned, however: replacing jumping with sitting takes lots of time and practice before the dog will do it on his own. Practise in short, frequent sessions, and as opportunities present themselves from day to day. Remember, preventing jumping as an option by putting your foot on the lead will help your dog to learn more quickly.

Plan Ahead for Success

If you want a well-trained dog that responds to your commands everywhere, you have to train it in all situations. Dogs pick things up quickly, but have a tendency to revert back to old, ingrained habits in new environments. If you haven't taught your dog to sit when greeting strangers in the park, he will not try that as his first choice of actions. Always be ready to reinforce the right behaviour and prevent the wrong one from happening as best you can. Have a lead hanging by the door so that you are ready to prevent jumping on guests, and have a container of treats ready to reinforce sitting.

tips

In order for the new training to replace old, well-established behaviour, it must be heavily reinforced with things that the dog finds rewarding. A reward can come in the form of attention, a game, an opportunity, or a treat – anything that the dog considers worthwhile.

If you're not prepared to train him, don't allow your dog to greet the visitor. If you want to cure deep-rooted behaviour, you have to combat it with well-timed repetitions, a high rate of rewards and frequent practice around distractions. It may seem awkward at first to carry your clicker and treats with you all the time, but it is essential to capture the moment when your dog makes the right choice.

Overall, training this way is more like real life for the dog, and the learning tends to become more permanent because the dog begins to realize that the commands work everywhere. The more distractions he has when practising, the quicker he will learn to respond to your commands in all places and situations.

Labrador Cross and Golden Retriever bow together

Control the Situation

Controlling the situation means controlling what's distracting your dog's attention from you. Distractions often ruin the best-laid plans simply because they are too stimulating for the dog to ignore. If you control the frequency, type and distance of the distractions, you will increase the speed with which your dog learns. If ringing the doorbell sends your dog into a frenzy, you may want to work on desensitizing him to the doorbell sound first; then you can move on to actually greeting the visitor. In this example, the dog's response to the doorbell and the dog's response to the person would be considered two separate issues.

Other distractions might include things that move, such as balls, off-lead dogs, cars, kids, runners or environmental factors – being outside, or the presence of food. The key points to keep in mind for getting your dog to be successful in these situations are controlling the distance between your dog and the distraction, and controlling the intensity of the distraction. For your dog's training programme to be successful, you need to find your dog's critical distance, and work from there.

How does 'critical distance' relate to training a dog?
The critical distance is the amount of distance between the dog and the distraction that must be present in order for him to behave well regularly. If he is too close to the distraction, it will be difficult for him to pay attention, and he will be less likely to respond to the command.

The distance at which he notices the distraction but will still perform the action is the starting point. Then, in subsequent training sessions, decrease that distance until he is able to work while the distractions are close by. You will immediately notice that the distance between your dog and the action is an important factor in the success of your training sessions. If the dog is overstimulated by the distraction, he will not be able to ignore it and will not perform the actions you ask him to do.

The second point to keep in mind when working around disturbances is to pay attention to how much of a distraction there is. To decrease the intensity of distraction, make sure there is less movement, fewer dogs, people, children or other visual stimuli before attempting to teach the dog anything. As your dog starts to learn to ignore distractions and perform the action well, you can gradually increase the intensity of training until he is working in the middle of the disturbance.

As you train your dog to respond to you regardless of where you are and what is happening, your aim over time is to decrease the distance and increase the intensity of the distractions so that your dog will pay attention to you and respond to you regardless of what else is going on.

Doing this in a slow sequence of progressions will help you attain your goals more quickly and reliably.

Prevention Is Half the Cure

It is human nature to notice what is going wrong and point it out. When trying to change behaviour in animals, putting pressure upon an animal to change the choices it has made is a waste of time, since the animal cannot change the past any more than you can.

Remember that prevention can come in the form of a lead, a crate, a gate or an extending lead – anything that keeps the dog from doing the wrong actions while you teach him an alternate response.

If you want to make a difference in future behaviour, you must set up the animal for success. Setting up an animal for success means limiting his options, providing good consequences for the correct choices and preventing or providing negative consequences for the wrong choices. Because the animal has choices, the learning is more permanent and the consequences will directly shape his response.

Pointing out a mistake acts as reinforcement and can actually teach the person or animal to make that same mistake over and over again. A much better approach to changing behaviour permanently is to avoid reinforcing the wrong behaviour in the first place and, if possible, preventing it from actually happening. It is important during the teaching phase to avoid giving the dog any attention for the wrong actions, and concentrate on noticing what's going right. This also means that you should be ready to reward unexpected good behaviour any time it happens. If you're not prepared to click and treat, then shower your dog with lots of praise and pats or games and opportunities.

Generalization... Taking It Into the World

Taking it into the world means getting your dog to respond to all of his commands in new environments by training your dog everywhere.

Generalization refers to the dog being able to perform the action each time, regardless of any distractions. Dogs need your help to get them on track in new environments.

The best way to help a dog whose behaviour falls apart in a new environment is to go back to nursery school. Help the dog perform the action with a treat or toy as a lure. The idea is to drill the dog for 5–10 repetitions to get him working again, and then to wean him off the extra help. Repeating the command when the dog is obviously too distracted to hear what you are saying is not teaching the dog anything but how to ignore you. With a little patience and practice, it won't be long before your dog understands that his training works everywhere, regardless of the distraction.

When teaching your dog to generalize his behaviour, a good rule of thumb is to give only one command. If the dog doesn't respond appropriately, get out a treat and help the dog do the action. Repeated commands will teach your dog a slower response to commands in public places.

Solutions to Specific Breed Behaviour Problems

Dogs with persistent behaviour problems are often exhibiting behaviour that is related to the job they were bred to do. When a dog has a behaviour problem related to its original working ability, think of it as atavistic behaviour, or behaviour that a dog's genetics have preprogrammed him to do. Consider the Border Collie that chases and nips at heels, the Retriever obsessed with having everything in his mouth, or the terrier that barks or chases squirrels. In these cases, the genetics of the dog determine his behaviour, because it is behaviour that the dog was bred to do, such as herding, retrieving, guarding or chasing things that move.

Constant and Patient Reinforcement

What atavism means for you is that without the appropriate training and practice, it will be harder to stop the dog from doing the undesirable actions.

There are several things to keep in mind when you are retraining dogs of this kind:

· Keep the rate of reinforcement high.
· Build up your dog's savings account for good behaviour.
· Train your dog to perform the action for a longer period of time.
· Consider teaching a trick as replacement behaviour.

If you are going to change the dog's mind about behaviour that is this instinctive, you need to provide lots of reinforcement for the actions you are trying to teach instead. A high rate of reinforcement means that you keep your standards low and reward the dog for even attempting the new action. You don't raise your standards or expect multiple repetitions; you simply reward the new action as often as possible. This way it will be more likely for your dog to respond to a situation with the right behaviour, because it has been rewarded so frequently.

Savings in the bank is each click and treat for the right behaviour. No one can ever have too much positive reinforcement for good behaviour. When you are trying to change atavistic behaviour, you must increase the likelihood of the right behaviour by making sure the bank account is full.

Each reward for the new behaviour is money in the bank. You are building a reinforcement history that has to compete with natural and self-rewarding behaviour. Building a strong reinforcement history takes time and practice before it will eventually replace the old, atavistic behaviour with the new, desirable one.

Practice Makes Perfect

The more you work with your dog, the fewer behaviour problems you will have. You are spending time building up a history of 'training equals fun!' Teaching your dog to perform tricks is a great way to help you get to know your dog and improve your relationship with him; in addition, training tricks is fun, and most people enjoy spending time training their dogs this way.

Golden
Retriever
takes a
German
Shepherd for
a walk

Some dogs love learning tricks more than anything else, so they are more willing to work longer and perform with enthusiasm. If you prefer to teach your dog tricks, why not use them in everyday life to help prevent your dog from practising inappropriate behaviour? If your dog pulls on the lead, how about mixing in Roll Overs, Sit Up or Spin to encourage the dog to stay with you. In order to use tricks to replace problem behaviour, not only does the dog have to know the trick very well in all different kinds of environments, he also has to be heavily rewarded (at least initially) for choosing to perform the trick rather than the inappropriate behaviour. The more you practise what you want, the better it will happen for you when you truly need it. The more creative you are in your training programme, the better your relationship with your dog will be.

The Bark Stops Here!

Barking can be a major issue in any neighbourhood (see Chapter 12). What is more maddening than listening to non-stop barking from a dog whose careless owner has tied him up and left him for hours? The dog's reasons for barking will determine what solution will work for your dog. Try to identify whether the dog is bored, unsocialized, nervous or just too exuberant; then try different approaches to see what works best for you and your dog. Some options to consider:

· Hide treat-stuffed Kong toys all over the garden to prevent boredom.
· Teach your dog to retrieve a toy and carry it to a visitor to help keep your dog quiet.
· Teaching your dog to Roll Over will use up some of the energy focused on barking.
· Teaching your dog to Spin will keep him too busy to bark.
· Asking for a play Bow is a nice greeting for an elderly person or a small child.
· For dogs that like to use their paws, teaching him to Wave will direct his energy appropriately.

Training your dog to perform an alternative action will do wonders in the way of doggie PR. It will make your guests comfortable, keep you calm and give everyone reason to reinforce your dog's good behaviour with lots of love and attention.

The best way to get rid of a barking problem is to recognize when the dog is about to erupt, and to interrupt and redirect his behaviour towards a more appropriate end.

Mugging Visitors at the Door

Jumping is a problem most dogs do not outgrow. Dogs mainly jump in their exuberance to greet a person and to welcome them to play. Teaching your dog alternative greeting behaviour may be an excellent solution for the jumping-on-people problems.

- Require a Sit/Stay or Down/Stay from the dog before people are allowed to pet him.
- Ask your dog to Play Dead or Belly Up and let the visitor scratch his belly as a reward.
- Teaching your dog to Roll Over and Spin, one straight after the other, is an excellent way to keep even the most energetic dog focused on his job of greeting sanely.
- Get your dog to fetch a toy, both to keep his mouth busy and his feet off the visitors.
- A Go to Bed and Stay command can save his life by keeping him away from the open door and the big wide world beyond.

Although there is no quick solution to jumping, preventing it from happening in the first place is a good start towards changing your dog's first response towards visitors. Remember that dogs do what works. If something is no longer an option, it is eliminated from the list of possibilities and is eventually replaced by what does work. Make sure that behaviour that works for your dog is something that works for you, too!

Who's Walking Who?

Pulling on the lead is by far the number one complaint from dog owners and the reason that they bring their dog to obedience class. Adding tricks to your dog's repertoire will help you manage his on-lead behaviour and give you more options when he starts pulling. If he never knows what you might ask him to do next, he'll be more likely to pay attention to you and less likely to pull.

Teaching your dog appropriate lead manners can be time-consuming and tedious; try breaking it up a little with some of these ideas:

- Play the targeting game as you walk by having your dog touch your hand or trouser leg with his nose as you walk along.

- While you are walking, stop every so often and ask your dog to Spin.
- Don't walk a long distance in one go without changing direction or frequently stopping to get your dog to Sit.
- Mix up moving with Stop and Wave.
- Stop every so often and ask your dog to Roll Over several times in a row; this will take the edge off an excitable dog.

Using tricks while teaching your dog to remain under control on the lead is an excellent way for him to learn to control his enthusiasm. Directing his energy towards more appropriate behaviour will teach him to pay attention to you and what you are asking him to do. Remember that your dog has been pulling you along behind him for a long time. Since there is a lot of money in your dog's savings account for pulling, you'll need to counter that with huge rewards for *not* pulling. This requires frequent practice and a commitment to make sure you don't follow your dog when he is pulling you.

Fierce or Nervous

Aggression and nervousness are two behaviour problems that are stressful for both the dog and the handler. Keeping your dog from becoming too overwhelmed and getting his attention back on you is your primary aim as the owner of a nervous or aggressive dog. Keep in mind that your ultimate goal is to give your dog a better association between the things he is afraid of and positive reinforcement. What better way to do that than to teach him to do tricks in situations where he normally reacts aggressively or timidly?

- Teach him to look at you for an extended period of time on command.
- Teach him to touch your hand with his nose.
- Teach him to touch an object or a person's hand (this has to be built up to slowly).
- Teach him to Spin or turn around.
- Teach him to Bow; this may help to lighten up dogs that are passing by and help your dog to feel more relaxed with their presence.

- Teach him to Wave.
- Teach him to Roll Over, which will disorient him enough for him not to know where the scary person or dog disappeared to by the time he's finished.
- Teach him to say Sorry, which will flatten him into a very submissive position – a great way to diffuse other dogs' aggression.

The purpose of teaching tricks to a nervous or aggressive dog is that when a dog is performing tricks – and is trained to ignore distractions – he is concentrating on something else. Think of this as another form of 'incompatible behaviour'.

Knowing exactly what your dog needs as a distraction is a better, more permanent way to get rid of behaviour problems. Noting what is going right and rewarding it will make it more likely that your dog will replace his old habits with more appropriate good dog manners. Remember that what you pay attention to is what you get; if you start ignoring what is going wrong and start rewarding what is going right, the behaviour you see as problems now will disappear, and you will be rewarded with a better-behaved companion.

CHAPTER 12

Barking Problems and Solutions

D ogs bark to communicate with us and with each other, but excessive barking is inappropriate and symptomatic of a larger problem. If a dog barks excessively it means that the dog's mental, emotional and physical needs are not being met. This problem must be addressed first, before peace and quiet can reign.

Why Do Dogs Bark Excessively?

A barking dog is a common problem among dog owners and is often the top complaint of neighbours who listen to the restless protests of a dog confined to a garden and bored to death. Dogs are pack animals with strong bonds to their family members; it is unnatural for them to be alone for hours at a time. In their boredom and frustration they tend to bark, which is self-reinforcing. Barking is an emotional release, a way for a dog to express emotion and let out bottled-up anxiety and frustration.

A dog that barks too much falls into one of three categories: the dog that barks when left alone; the dog that barks at visitors, noise and people passing by while you are home; and lastly the dog that barks at you for attention. Excessive barking is a symptom of a larger issue. In general, it means that the dog needs something that he isn't getting or is being consistently rewarded for the wrong behaviour.

Meet Your Dog's Needs

All dogs need a healthy diet, a predictable schedule, lots of exercise, interaction with people and other dogs, training, a safe place to sleep and rest, and a stimulating environment with toys and things to chew. Dogs also need to be taught from the time they are puppies to be content when they are away from you, so that they come to expect that you will return at predictable intervals to take care of their needs.

Just like people, well-adjusted dogs are happy. Finding a healthy balance between time alone and time with people is essential for the emotional well-being of any dog.

Dogs that are with their owners all the time (perhaps you work from home or are a stay-at-home parent) can also become excessive barkers when their owners leave them, even briefly. These dogs become inappropriately bonded to their owners and in their absence find it difficult to cope with being alone. This overattachment between owner and dog can erode the dog's self-confidence and contentment when he is alone. Take a moment to examine how much or how little time you spend with your dog, and then make the necessary adjustments to help him feel confident and secure.

Mindful Management

The next few sections review some basic elements of what you need to keep in mind while you come up with a plan to silence (or at least cut down) your dog's barking. The philosophy is the same for training any wrong behaviour: have a plan, be patient, be consistent and reward the right actions.

Doing What Comes Naturally

Some breeds are prone to barking, but all dogs can learn not to bark excessively or inappropriately. If you have a dog that is known for barking, nip the problem in the bud while the dog is still a puppy. Some dogs were bred for their ability to chase or guard, and barking is sometimes still part of the package.

Thinking creatively about changing your dog's environment may give you a little more peace and quiet. Think about planting a row of bushes in your front garden, or close the front curtains or blinds to block your dog's view of the neighbourhood.

If you know what sets your dog off into a frenzy of barking, think carefully about how you can prevent these episodes from happening. The more barking your dog does, the more excitable he is likely to become. The more agitated a dog becomes, the more likely the behaviour is to occur and become stronger. If you want to have a quieter household, you need to find your dog's triggers for barking and short-circuit as many of them as you can.

Set a Reasonable Goal

A dog that barks a lot isn't going to just stop one day when you find the magic cure. Barking is a habit with dogs, and often gets worse before it gets better. First, sit down with your family and set a reasonable goal for your dog. Perhaps your dog is the type that barks when the doorbell

Hound Cross barking

rings; in this case, your goal might be that he's allowed to bark for 30 seconds, and then he must be quiet when you tell him to be quiet. Alternatively, if he hears a noise, he can let you know something's going on, but then he must stop barking and go to his bed. It really doesn't matter what the target is, so long as it is simple and fairly easy for the dog to do.

It is your job to sit down, agree on something reasonable and teach it to the dog. Don't be afraid to set small goals and build up the time the dog is required to be quiet by seconds. It isn't reasonable to expect a dog that has been barking excessively for years to suddenly stop overnight.

Find the Antecedents of Barking

An antecedent is the trigger or the cause of an action. For instance, your dog barks at the sound of a knock or the doorbell. The knock or doorbell would be considered the antecedent for the action of barking. Knowing what triggers your dog's barking can be crucial to teaching him to be quiet. The pattern or chain of reaction goes like this: antecedent, action, training, appropriate behaviour, reward. You need to complete this entire circuit of behaviour in order to teach your dog not to bark excessively.

A good way to find antecedents is to keep a chart of when your dog barks and what happens immediately before he barks. Write down exactly what you think triggered the barking, and time how long it took him to stop. If you time how long it takes your dog to calm down, you will know when you are making progress in your training programme and when you are making real progress. You'll know you're on track if the number of seconds it takes your dog to calm down becomes smaller over time. Good dog trainers keep a chart of their progress to see results!

To change your dog's response to a typical antecedent to barking, such as the doorbell, ring the doorbell at random times and give the dog a handful of delicious treats or play a favourite game like tug or fetch. Your ignoring both the bell and the door will teach your dog an alternative expectation to doorbell ringing.

Set the Consequences

For dogs that keep on and on and barely take a breath between barks, you may want to use something to interrupt the barking. This way you will be stopping the barking for a second so that you can reward him for being quiet. A consequence is the same as punishment, so alone it will only stop the behaviour – it will not teach the dog what he should do instead.

Some ideas for training might be a squirt of water, a loud noise, shaking a tin of coins or a non-electric no-bark collar (this device is worn around the neck and distracts the dog by squirting a blast of citronella when he barks). Consequences would be used to interrupt the action of excessive barking to get the dog to stop for a second so that he could be rewarded for being quiet. You will want to plan in advance what the dog should do instead of bark so that you know what behaviour to reward.

If you just correct the dog for barking and fail to reward it for being quiet, you will get a dog that eventually goes back to barking because it isn't being rewarded for anything else. Remember that what gets rewarded gets repeated.

Notice the Right Things

Too often with a noisy dog, we tend to notice only when they are barking and not when they are quiet. A good part of the solution for barking is catching and rewarding the dog for being quiet. Each reward you provide for quiet behaviour will be money in the bank towards having a quieter dog overall. Pay attention to your dog at times such as this by petting or playing with him, giving a treat, bringing him inside, letting him outside, opening the crate door and so on. Whatever would be rewarding at the moment, treat your dog with it and you will notice that your dog barks less over the course of several days or weeks (depending on the value of the reward and the severity of the problem).

Remember that barking is just like any bad habit; it is easier to slip back into old patterns of behaviour because they are familiar and sometimes rewarding. Management and prevention are critical.

Set for Success

If you live in a busy neighbourhood, get smart – letting your dog have unsupervised free access to your garden is not a good idea. He will only find things to bark at, effectively reinforcing his obnoxious behaviour over and over. This poor management is money in the bank for more barking, because dogs think that barking is fun and will continue to do so in the absence of anything better to occupy their time. Setting up your dog to succeed means that you use prevention to help your dog to be quiet, and then make sure you notice and reward him for *being* quiet. Following are some tips for setting your dog up to succeed.

Exercise. A dog can never have too much. Try games with other dogs, games of fetch, Frisbee, hide-and-seek, day care kennels, pet sitters, dog walkers or anyone who will exercise your dog for you.

Occupation. Try interesting toys, bones and chew treats that let your dog exercise his jaws. Dogs that bark are often big chewers, so make sure your dog has plenty of good things to chew.

Pay attention. Be there to supervise and redirect your dog. When you are present in the garden, for instance, practise calling your dog away from what he is barking at and reward him when he does come to you.

Keep him busy. Stuff hollow toys with peanut butter and dry dog food, and hide them all over the house and garden; this will give him something to do while you are out.

Remove the antecedent. Prevent barking as often as possible by blocking his view with shrubs, closing the curtains or rearranging the furniture. Not allowing your dog to continue the wrong actions is more than half the cure.

Meet his needs. Make a schedule and stick to it as much as possible. Hire a professional dog walker or leave him at a day kennel to help you with walks and exercise if necessary. The more predictable your dog's routine, the better it is for him. Try to feed, walk and play with your dog on a predictable schedule so that he will learn to trust you and feel secure.

Be ready. It is very important to be ready to reinforce what's going right. Make a plan with your family, and stick to it. The more you know what you want, the more likely you are to get it.

Use a marker signal. The use of a clicker to identify for the dog which behaviour is rewardable (the quiet behaviour) is crucial information for the dog, and it is difficult to provide it in any other way. Remember that the click marks the quiet behaviour so you can then follow through with the reward.

Dogs That Bark at Visitors

Dogs that go berserk over visitors may be nervous, overexcited or plain aggressive to people entering your home. Trying to train the dog to like visitors while also trying to greet your guest is dangerous, and will probably be only limitedly successful. A new pattern of training is necessary to teach the dog to respond to visitors in a more appropriate way.

If your dog is aggressive or nervous of strangers, you will probably want to enlist the help of a qualified professional dog trainer or behaviourist to help you evaluate your dog and correctly identify the problem. This person will also help you set up training sessions to help your dog learn better greeting manners and be safe doing it. The biggest task is to change your dog's mind about how he feels about visitors.

1. Put the dog out of the room and let your visitors come in and sit down.
2. After about 10 minutes, let your dog out and get everyone to ignore him.
3. Arm each person with tasty treats, and get the visitors to drop those treats all around their feet.
4. Let your dog be the one to go to the visitor to take the treats.

Congratulations! You have just performed your first step forward in stopping barking at visitors. Repeat this as often as you can with lots of different people until your dog begins to look forward to having visitors at the door. You may want to practise this scenario with your own family first, to teach the dog this new pattern of behaviour and to help the family members learn a new way of managing the dog when visitors come.

To speed up your dog's learning, leave a basket of your dog's favourite toys outside your front door so that visitors are armed with a toy as soon as you open the door. This will distract your dog from barking and help him develop a new habit in greeting guests at the door.

If you're not prepared to train your dog on a given occasion, remove him from the stimuli so at least you're not reinforcing the old pattern of behaviour and losing ground. Putting the dog in a separate room or his crate will at least make sure he doesn't fall back into his old ways.

Friendly Options

Dogs that bark because they are happy to see company simply need a distraction to keep them quiet. Teaching your dog to pick up a stuffed toy on his way to the door will keep his mouth busy and make it impossible for him to bark and hold the toy at the same time. This is what is meant by teaching your dog to do something that is incompatible with barking. A dog can't bark with a toy in his mouth.

You'll want to make sure it's a toy he really loves so that he'll want to hold the toy more than he'll want to bark. You can even leave a basket of toys by the door and let your visitor select one to greet your dog with. This will teach your dog that visitors are fun but that barking isn't part of that fun. Take advantage of any willing helpers, such as neighbours, fellow dog lovers and friends. The more your dog gets to practise greeting guests quietly, the better for everyone. Take your time and experiment with different toys to see which ones become your dog's favourites and keep him so engrossed that he forgets to bark!

Taming Doorbell Madness

Dogs that burst into action at the sound of the doorbell will need some help in getting over this huge stimulus before they can be expected to be quiet. The sound of the doorbell ringing may be your dog's antecedent to barking and the most difficult of distractions for him. Most dogs with this problem explode into a cacophony of shrill barking and take several minutes to calm down.

What is the difference between operant and classical conditioning?
Operant conditioning (click and treat) recognizes, and therefore encourages, desired behaviour. Classical conditioning creates positive associations between two events.

The best way to manage these dogs is to teach them an alternative response to the ringing doorbell. The easiest and noisiest way to do this is through a process called 'flooding'. This involves ringing the doorbell a billion times when no one is there for the dog to greet, so that it eventually doesn't mean what the dog thinks it means. He will start to develop an alternative response to the doorbell and come to expect something different from what he originally thought.

You can also add a bit of classical conditioning to change the dog's relationship with the doorbell. This conditioning is about developing associations between a noise or object, in this case the doorbell, and something good, like a treat or a game of fetch. To incorporate conditioning into the training, ring the bell and shower the dog with treats or start throwing a ball around, regardless of the dog's behaviour (barking or not).

Here, we are not requiring the dog to do something before he gets something, as in operant conditioning or clicker training. To the novice trainer, it may seem at first that we are rewarding the dog for barking when we ring the bell and treat the dog. In reality we are trying to form an association between the doorbell and something good so that eventually, instead of barking, your dog will be expecting a treat – perhaps a game, a toy or a pat from the visitor. This can be a very powerful tool in trying to change your dog's association with doorbells. Using it to help solve your barking problem may get you where you want to go faster than through other methods.

Dogs That Bark for Attention

Some dogs have their owners completely sussed. Remember that most dogs don't work for a living and have nothing else to do but sit around and watch you. They know just what to do to get what they want by barking at you until they get it. When a dog barks at you for attention, it usually means that he is confused about who's in charge in the family, and he may not have enough rules and limits put upon him to give him a clue as to where he falls in the family hierarchy.

Is there a trick to getting the dog to stop barking for attention?
It is important that everyone in the family is committed to ignoring the dog when he is barking for attention and definitely does not give in to the dog's demands. The more the habit of barking at people for attention doesn't work, the faster this problem behaviour will disappear.

The one thing that almost always works for these attention-seeking dogs is to stop paying attention to them when they are barking and to start noticing, acknowledging and rewarding them for being quiet. Walk away and turn your head to the side, or turn your back on your dog to let him know that what he is doing is not rewardable. If your dog is used to getting his way by barking, this method of management may take a while, but overall it is a faster process and more productive than constantly yelling at the dog to be quiet.

Head Halters

There are several types of training equipment available from pet shops and at vets' that you can use to shorten your training time by gently helping your dog relax and trust that you are in charge. The Halti head halter is one of these. Head halters are excellent equipment to own, and with the proper introduction, they will cut your training time in half (see Chapter 15).

Introduce the head halter slowly and with lots of treats and positive associations. The more positively you introduce your dog to this piece of equipment, the more useful it will be to you. If you rush it, your dog's resistance will make the halter a hindrance rather than a help.

The original purpose of the head halter is to teach dogs not to pull, by guiding them under the chin. In essence, when a dog is wearing one of these, you control his forward movement by controlling his head. The head halter has an added benefit, too: when fitted correctly, it puts gentle pressure on two points on the dog's head and neck, which help the dog relax and make him feel more secure.

Some dogs find the effect so calming that they forget to bark and are overall more relaxed and mellow. Head halters should be introduced very slowly if they are to be a useful tool for you. Dogs need to be taught to wear a head halter, but once they like wearing them, it can have an amazing effect on their behaviour.

Canine Massage

An often-overlooked method of achieving a quieter dog is canine massage. The massage technique most worthy of mention for changing unwanted behaviour is called Tellington Touch, or T-touch. It was started on horses by an American, Linda Tellington-Jones, and has been applied to all kinds of animals for all kinds of behaviour problems.

Dogs hold a lot of their emotions in their face and mouth area, and most dogs that are tense or hyperactive tend to bark and chew to relieve anxiety. In general, dogs that are restless, overactive, aggressive or excessive barkers often have a chewing or biting problem as well. These animals can benefit from a bit of therapeutic massage on their muzzle and gum line.

The best T-touch technique involves making small circles on the muzzle and jaw line with the tips of the forefingers and middle fingers. You'll want to lightly move the skin in a clockwise direction for a full circle, then move your hand up and do another circle right next to it. Take your time, and massage each circle for a count of five – and remember to breathe.

Where can you find more information on the T-touch technique?
See Appendix A for references.

You may want to start getting your dog used to this by sitting on a chair or the floor and getting your dog to sit between your feet. Support under his jaw with one hand while you make circles with the other. Use a light pressure, about as much as would be comfortable if you made a circle on your eyelid. You can even slip your finger under the dog's lip and make small circles on the gum line itself. You may want to wet your fingers first if your dog has a dry mouth.

There's Always Hope for the Problem Barker

Barking can be problematic for owners and neighbours alike, but it doesn't have to be. Owning a pet should be an enjoyable experience, and barking should not get in the way of you and your family enjoying your pet: the time to act is now. The longer you let your dog reward himself by getting what he wants when he barks, the more barking you will have to listen to over the months and years.

Put together a training plan that will help change your barking lunatic into the quiet companion you've always wanted. You have the tools to change the behaviour; now it's time to get to work. Take time to look seriously at the ways in which you are meeting your dog's basic needs for exercise – changing this by increasing your dog's playtime with other dogs is often a huge factor in cutting down on the amount of barking you have to listen to. Most of all, don't give up. Even the most obnoxious barker can be taught to be a quieter, more enjoyable companion; he just needs to be trained.

CHAPTER 13

Fears and Phobias

A nervous dog is a challenge to own and train. In familiar surroundings, he is a sweet, wonderful family pet, but in new places where there are strange sounds and people, he turns into a mess of jittery, shaking nerves. If you own a dog like this, it is important to educate yourself and learn all you can, in order to help your dog become a less nervous and more confident companion.

Make a Commitment to Training

Nervous dogs do not suddenly become confident, even with lots of training. Training a timid dog to be more confident is a time-consuming project that is best undertaken with a determined attitude and clear, achievable target-setting. Being specific about how you want your dog to react and behave is a huge step towards making it a reality.

Nervous dogs operate on emotions; they are not really thinking about what they are doing, and therefore no amount of correction or comforting will help them get over it and act as they do at home. If you take on the project of working with a dog like this, you will have to learn to be patient and flexible.

When training a timid dog, it is important to be flexible; you will not always move in a forwards direction. Sometimes it will feel like you move one step forwards and ten steps back. Being flexible enough to realize when you've pushed too hard, and being intuitive enough to know what changes to make so that your dog is successful are two of the most important elements of a successful dog trainer.

Miniature Pinscher 'peeping' out from under a blanket

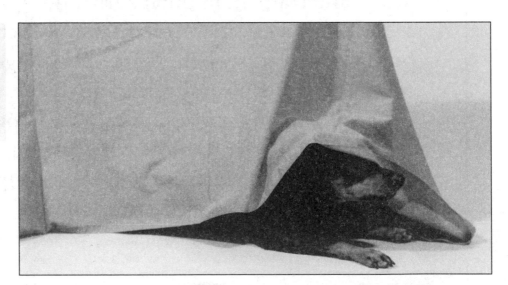

Be Organized and Consistent

Having a regular schedule of training is important in training any dog, but it is absolutely critical when working with a dog that is nervous. Breaking your training down into steps is the key to seeing improvement in a relatively short period of time. For instance, perhaps your dog is afraid of strange men. You may start off by using a male member of your family that your dog likes and teaching your dog to target the person's hand (see Chapter 4).

Targeting involves the dog approaching the strange person and touching his nose to the person's hand. This training, of course, would need to be broken down into really tiny pieces if the dog is really afraid of the strange person. For instance, you may want to get the person to sit in a chair and ignore the dog at first. Then you could ask the stranger to drop small pieces of treats all around his feet and let your dog take his time about going up and eating them. If your dog is too scared to eat, break it down into something even easier, like getting the person to lie on the sofa or sit a greater distance away. Your dog's appetite is a good indicator to his comfort level. If he is too stressed to eat, you need to make changes in order to see any progress.

The amount of time you spend training your dog to target will really pay off when you start to apply it in the situations where the dog is afraid. The training of targeting becomes a game to the dog if you practise enough.

You then gradually change the training so that the dog is able to eventually go and target the person's hand for a click and treat. Most people who have been successful using targeting to teach their dog to get over their fears have done an extensive amount of training, teaching their dogs to target their own hands and the hands of people the dog likes. Targeting can also be used to teach your dog to learn to be brave around scary objects or to learn to jump into the car or bath.

You will find that because targeting has such good associations for your dog, he will be more willing to extend himself and be open to new experiences; it will give him something to do instead of being scared. Taking the time to teach your dog how to target will be one of the most important training tools you have to help your dog get over his fears.

Genetics, Abuse or a Lack of Exposure?

People often assume that nervous dogs have been mistreated by a prior owner or some other person who has had contact with the dog. More commonly, however, dogs are timid or phobic because they lack early experience with many different types of people, sounds and experiences, including other dogs. Genetics can also play a fairly large role in shaping a dog's nervous behaviour, and some breeds have shyness as a common, if undesirable, trait.

It is very important to research who you are buying your puppy from, and to steer clear of puppy farms, pet shops and places where they breed more than one breed.

Breeding

A good breeder is committed to turning out puppies that are healthy, well-adjusted and ready for life. They screen their potential puppy buyers, and make sure that they educate each person who buys a puppy so that the training and socialization of the puppies is appropriate. The reality is that you get what you pay for, and quality puppies from good breeders don't come cheap. A lot of love and care goes into each puppy if the breeder does his or her job right.

If you feel your dog's problems stem from a genetic component, it is still possible to train him. Even in well-bred dogs with conscientious breeders, some puppies can be more timid than their littermates. If the shyness is identified early enough and intensive socialization and training is implemented, a lot of progress can be made in a relatively short period of time. The earlier the problem is identified, the better the prognosis. Certain breeds can be more prone to nerves, but any dog can grow up being timid and suspicious of new people and experiences.

The puppy aptitude test is a series of tests performed on 49-day-old puppies that helps determine their tendencies to be outgoing, shy, mischievous or pushy. More information on puppy aptitude testing can be obtained from DogWise, a dog and cat book retailer, which can be found online at *www.dogwise.com*.

A genetic predisposition to noise sensitivity is common in many breeds used for hunting and sporting purposes. Dog breeders who truly care will breed out these traits by choosing only the friendliest, most confident dogs for their breeding programmes. If you are looking for a puppy of a breed that has nervous tendencies, ask lots of questions about the parents' temperaments, meet both parents before purchasing the pup and choose a breeder who has had a vet check the puppies in all their litters. Dogs that are carefully bred by knowledgeable, caring people should be friendly and outgoing, regardless of breed.

Social Development

If you feel your dog's nervousness is a result of a lack of early socialization, and your dog is still under a year old, get out there and get busy. The earlier you start to change this, the more successful your training programme is likely be. Conversely, the longer you wait, the harder it will be to change.

Consider enrolling your dog in a well-organized group training class. Be honest with your instructor about what your aims are, and ask if a group class would be an appropriate place to start with your dog. Consider a dog handler in your area; there are probably several who take on special cases and who are knowledgeable about these problems. They can help make sure your dog has an enjoyable time. Don't be afraid to ask questions, and be flexible and consistent with your part of the commitment to training.

Getting a puppy from a breeder who has been raising dogs for many years and with knowledge of how to provide the right kind of environment will save you years of time in the long run. If a puppy misses out on these critical early social periods and is not raised in an environment that stimulates him to explore and learn about his world, he will be a nervous, phobic adult dog. Shyness, fears and fear-related aggression are probably the result of a lack of socialization rather than past abuse or mistreatment. Often abuse is used as the excuse for dogs that are timid or aggressive, when in reality it is a lack of early socialization that is the problem. However, there are dogs out there that have been mistreated and are nervous and skittish as a result of learning that strange people and places are scary and dangerous. The same advice applies if your dog has been mistreated; sit down and develop a plan, and then get out there and train your dog!

Young puppies have a critical window of socialization from eight to about 18 weeks old. Socialization doesn't end at 18 weeks, of course, but if the right amount has not been given, it will have serious side effects on a puppy's overall temperament and confidence.

Now Get Busy Training

All dogs need structure, but nervous dogs need even more. The more predictable the schedule and house rules, the better able they will be to cope with life. Spoiling or indulging these dogs will make them worse, because above all else, a timid dog needs a strong, fair and consistent leader. Providing structure for a nervous dog means feeding, walking and exercising him at specific times. It means having house rules that are hardly ever broken, such as no dogs on the bed, dog must sit before going outside, having his dish put on the floor or having his lead put on.

No matter what your house rules are, the most important thing is that you have them. A dog that knows what is expected of him will know that you are the head of the household. This alone will give him more confidence. House rules can be flexible, but not until your dog is more confident. The more strict and consistent the rules are, the quicker the dog will be to trust that you can take care of him, and the more he will look to you for leadership.

Establish Rules

There are several things you can do to help raise your dog's confidence level and make it more likely that your training programme will be successful in the end.

Avoid reinforcing nervous behaviour. Petting and talking soothingly to the dog or picking him up reinforces the dog for the nervous behaviour. A hands-off approach, where you state that everything is fine, will send the message to your dog that there is really nothing to fear.

No punishment – ever! There is never a reason for punishment in a situation where a dog is nervous. If a dog is frightened, he is in an emotional state, not a learning state. Physical or verbal correction will only convince him that there really is something to fear. Punishment may even bring out aggression if your dog feels threatened and vulnerable. Avoid any type of correction; it won't get you where you want to go.

Safety first. Keep the lead on at all times in public, and make all the exits in your house escape-proof. Deny your dog access to the front door, for instance, if he is constantly trying to dash out of the door, or if he has a tendency to panic during thunderstorms or at loud noises.

Exercise and mental stimulation. Dogs that lack confidence need exercise more than ever. Chasing a ball, hide-and-seek, learning tricks, agility, fly ball or any of the various dog sports are all excellent ways for your dog to release his energy reserves and the tensions of the day.

Paying attention to providing the right environment for your dog, and making sure that it is one in which he can learn to trust (because it is consistent and predictable) will put you on the road to helping your dog become a more confident and enjoyable companion.

Confidence Training

Nervous dogs don't have to stay that way forever. With lots of patience and careful training, you can help your dog enjoy life just a little more. Keep in mind, however, that building confidence in a timid dog is time-consuming; don't expect miracles overnight. Be flexible in your plans. Be sure to make room for regression, and have a plan as to how you will handle it. Being prepared for setbacks will also help your dog gain confidence more quickly, since his handler will simply try another approach and continue, rather than panicking and confusing him.

Teaching your dog to target and making a game out of it is a great way to build his confidence. If you practise enough, it becomes so second nature to the dog that he will learn to play it regardless of what else is going on around him. Teaching your dog to target your hand (see Chapter 4) involves your dog bumping your hand with his nose for a click and treat. This can be a powerful tool in building your dog's confidence. Making targeting a game will give you a tool to raise his confidence level regardless of the circumstances, but in order for it to be useful you must practise a lot.

Going slowly and building your dog's confidence gradually will pay dividends for less nervous behaviour. If you blow it and move too fast, go backwards and move more slowly, or just stop the session and try again another time.

Review the chapter on targeting, and once you've got your dog easily following your hand, transfer the target to another person. Find a helper that the dog knows, and have her offer her hand as a target for your dog to touch. You may have to go back to the early steps and get the helper to start off with a treat in her hand at first. Gradually increase the distance so that your dog will go across the room to touch the person's outstretched hand. Verbally name the action Say Hello. Congratulations!

You now have a new game to play with your dog and a way to increase his confidence around new people. Practise at every opportunity, and be sure to have a back-up plan in case he is too nervous to target. Having a back-up plan will make sure that your training session goes smoothly, and your dog will barely notice the change of plan.

Classical Conditioning

Using classical conditioning in your training programme can help you cover more ground quickly, because it deals more with associations and feelings than with actually requiring the dog to perform a certain action. Classical conditioning involves forming an association that 'scary thing' equals 'good stuff'. Good stuff can come in the form of games, toys, food, affection or anything the dog finds comforting. Using this technique can be helpful for dogs that are too scared to work at all, or for noise sensitivities and phobias.

Golden Retriever bowing

The way that classical conditioning works is that each time the noise is present, the treats shop is open. Throw treats on the ground, play ball or a favourite game. When the noise goes away, so does all the good stuff and your attention as well (ignore your dog for at least five minutes). Your aim is to change the dog's association with the feared noise to one of expecting good things to happen.

The most important thing to keep in mind with this type of training is that the dog gets good things regardless of his behaviour. Remember that you are trying to form an association between the scary person, noise or thing and things the dog likes.

Using classical conditioning on your way to trying to change your nervous dog's behaviour is like making huge bank deposits in your dog's savings bank account. It will complement your dog's operant training programme because you have a more relaxed dog to train. Half the problem of training a timid dog is that he is not relaxed enough to absorb the lesson and therefore requires a great deal more repetition and more changes of variables.

Systematic Desensitization

This technique involves playing a noise at a very low volume or keeping the scary person or thing at enough distance so that the dog notices it but does not react anxiously to it. A good rule of thumb is that if the dog won't take a treat or play with you, the volume is too high or the distance is too close. Increase the volume gradually, or bring the person or thing closer, so that eventually the dog will ignore it all together and continue to take treats and play.

The process of systematic desensitization involves interacting with the dog in a positive way, be it with a game of fetch or teaching tricks, so as to help the dog develop a more positive association with the feared noise. The dog starts to associate the feeling of being relaxed around the scary noise or object, and eventually the volume can be increased and the distance decreased until the dog will accept the new thing as part of his environment and no longer find it threatening.

Teaching tricks would be a great way for the dog to associate fun with noise. If you move slowly enough, you will find that having fun learning and performing tricks is incompatible with acting timid. With enough patience and practice, you will have a dog that is able to get over his fears because he has learned to trust that only good things happen.

Veterinary Behaviourists and Alternative Solutions

Veterinary behaviourists are skilled both as veterinarians and as dog behaviour experts. You may consider the help of a behaviourist to help diagnose your dog's problem and help you get started working towards a solution. The main difference between a veterinary behaviourist and a dog trainer/behaviourist is that the veterinary behaviourist can prescribe medication for dogs with problems that are too intense or severe to change with training alone.

Remember that nervous dogs didn't get that way overnight. A high rate of encouragement (frequent clicks and treats for anything that is going right) will help you build your dog's savings account for being confident, and this will help your dog get used to new people or things.

Consider seeking the help of a veterinary behaviourist if you don't seem to be making any progress over a six-week period, or if your dog seems unnaturally timid. Some dogs are so scared of being left alone that they will cause injury to themselves or major destruction to their surroundings in the absence of their owners. Dogs like this may benefit from veterinary-prescribed drugs that will help restore chemical balance and assist them in learning appropriate and alternative behaviour. If your dog suffers from a chemical imbalance, no amount of training will change that. Restoring the body to its equilibrium will ensure that your dog will be able to make the most of his training sessions and will make progress faster. In most cases, the goal is to wean the dog off the medication by adhering to a strict behaviour programme until the dog learns a new response.

Veterinary behaviourists also have experience with difficult or unusual problems, such as excessive tail-chasing, shadow-chasing, obsessive behaviour, severe separation anxiety and aggression. A veterinary behaviourist usually charges a substantial fee, which covers the initial visit, when the behaviourist will meet your dog and get a complete history in order to diagnose your dog's problem and advise you on treatment.

The behaviourist will probably design a training programme for you to follow, and ask you to give updates on your dog's progress. In some cases, the behaviourist may even refer you to a local obedience trainer to help coach you as you implement the training programme. Not all problems require medication, but in some severe cases pharmacological intervention can save you huge amounts of time in training and make the success of your training programme much more likely.

Natural Remedies

If you have a dog that has complex behaviour problems, it is crucial to keep an open mind about alternative methods of treatment. Not all solutions will seem to fit your problems or be something you may have even considered, such as massage, acupuncture or homeopathy.

Holistic veterinary practitioners may use alternative solutions for nervous dogs. Homeopathic remedies often work to help your dog restore his natural balance so that his body can heal itself. If you decide to go down this route, the veterinarian will take a detailed history of not only your dog's heath and diet but also his likes, dislikes and general behaviour issues. Consider seeking out a professional to consult, to see what recommendations she might have for your dog. She may use a combination of herbal remedies, body wraps, massage techniques and behaviour training to help you achieve your aim of a more confident pet. The more alternatives you seek, the more likely you are to find a solution that will help improve the speed of your dog's training programme.

Alternative Solutions

Fear is an emotion that can get in the way of training; because of this, you may find that training alone is not the entire solution. Consider seeking out alternative methods of treatment to be sure that you have checked everything. Often fears are the result of an injury or underlying medical problem that goes undetected and can often be successfully identified through chiropractic or acupuncture consultations.

There are also lots of different massage techniques available for dogs, including the Tellington Touch (see page 158). This type of technique helps dogs to become more confident and aware of their bodies, and works well in conjunction with a behaviour-modification programme. Regardless of what you start with, the general rule to keep in mind is that it can do no harm. The more open-minded you are about trying something new, the more your dog will benefit. If you have a difficult problem, the best approach is to seek out as much information as possible so that you have lots of tools to help your dog live a more comfortable life and make him a more enjoyable companion.

To find alternative practitioners, such as acupuncturists, chiropractors, massage therapists or other types of alternative specialists in your area, try asking other dog owners, looking in the Yellow Pages, asking at your local health food store, contacting the nearest veterinary practice or doing a search on the Internet.

In general, phobic dogs are a mix of unfortunate experiences and a lack of early socialization appropriate for their temperament. Retraining these dogs to be more confident can be a challenge. Changing behaviour that is based on fear isn't easy. It requires a huge commitment of time and energy to help your dog learn to cope with life, but the owners who embark on this adventure find the rewards immeasurable. If you are truly committed to making your dog a more confident and participating member of your family, start training your dog today!

CHAPTER 14

Housetraining

Housetraining problems are the leading cause of people giving up their animals to shelters. Nothing erodes the bond of human and dog quicker than a puddle or a pile on the carpet. Dogs have a natural housetraining instinct that involves sleeping in a place separate from where they urinate or defecate; we take advantage of this instinct when we housetrain them.

Why Things Go Wrong

In some cases, the puppy was not raised by a superclean mum that kept the whelping box free of stool. In other cases, the puppy may have spent too much time in a cage in a pet shop or a shelter, and learned to go in his crate because there was no other option. If the natural instinct to urinate or defecate away from the sleeping area is missing, it usually means that the puppy was mishandled and was not given the opportunity to go outside the sleeping area. A puppy that doesn't have this instinct can be a lot more difficult to housetrain. This doesn't mean he can't learn to go in the appropriate place, but it will mean that the whole process will take a little longer than average and require you to be more vigilant and flexible with your walking schedule.

Welsh Terrier checking the rubbish

Another problem with housetraining occurs when humans confuse setting limits with being mean or allowing too much freedom too soon. When pups have free run of the house, they do their toilet whenever they have to go; as a result, they never learn to hold it. Other pups are not supervised well enough when they do have freedom, and sneak off to 'go' somewhere inappropriate when no one is looking. Almost all housetraining problems are caused by human error, which is good news.

It means that all you need to do is educate yourself, so that you, too, can have a dog that knows where to do its toilet.

Using a Crate to Help Housetrain Your Dog

The dog's ancestor, the wolf, housetrained himself by sleeping in a cave and urinating and defecating outside that cave. Through the adult's example, the puppies learned to do the same. We mimic this cave concept when we crate- or cage-train our dogs. Using a crate is like giving your dog his own bedroom, a place for him to relax and rest without getting into trouble. Being confined to a crate requires him to hold his bladder and bowels to avoid an unpleasant consequence (having to sit in his own mess until you come to rescue him).

Using a crate gives a clear message to a puppy: 'Hold it until I let you out.' Such a message takes advantage of his natural instincts to sleep in one place and void in another. Using a crate is the nicest thing you can do for your dog, and if it's used properly it will help speed up housetraining. Following are some tips for using a crate:

1. A young puppy (less than 16 weeks) should be in the crate more than he is out, and should only be free when you are there to supervise him.
2. No food or water should be given in the crate while you are gone.
3. No towels or bedding in the crate at first until he's been dry in the crate for at least two weeks in a row. Otherwise, he may go on the towel and then kick it to the back.
4. A puppy between the ages of eight and 12 weeks will need to be taken to the potty-training spot, to see if he needs to go, every hour at first and then every two to three hours after that.
5. Hire a pet sitter to provide regular walks if you are gone for long periods during the day.
6. Puppies aged 12–18 weeks can last a bit longer between walks, but you should increase the time gradually.
7. If your puppy cries or barks in the crate, try to ignore him until he is quiet before letting him out. Covering the crate completely with

a sheet or towel often helps puppies settle down to sleep faster, especially if they bark and whine a lot.

8. When introducing the crate, leave the door open and entice your puppy in and out with treats or toys. You can also use the clicker and treats to help your puppy going in and out of the crate.

9. Put your puppy in the crate frequently when you are at home so that he gets used to being away from you for gradually longer periods of time.

10. Keep your crate around throughout the first and second years of your dog's life. You will find it a godsend if you have workmen doing repairs or people visiting, or if you travel with your dog. If you teach your dog to like his crate, he will always have a safe place to call his own, no matter where he goes.

Dogs that can't use a crate for whatever reason should be supervised constantly and not allowed free access to the rest of the house until they have been reliable with their housetraining for at least six weeks. Freedom after that should be given only gradually, until you are absolutely certain that your dog is reliable.

Crates are not just for housetraining – they also help keep your puppy safe while you are away, and prevent destructive chewing. Although the crate may not be useful to some people as a housetraining tool, you may find it extremely useful for getting through all of the destructive phases of your dog's development.

Charting Your Dog's Progress

Teaching a dog to use the outside for toilet training is not rocket science, but it can be frustrating and time-consuming. Some tricks about housetraining won't teach your dog to go outside overnight, but they will make sure that you are moving in that general direction. A really useful tool in housetraining a dog is to keep a chart that tracks what time he was walked, if he went, and what he did. A simple chart on the fridge will help the whole family keep track of your puppy's progress, and make it easier to know when your puppy can have some freedom and when he should be supervised carefully for signs that he has to go out (most puppies will sniff the floor and walk in circles when they need to go out).

Housetraining Habits

A young puppy of between seven and 12 weeks should be walked every hour. It is the repetition of being taken to the same spot time and again that gives him the idea of what he needs to do and where to do it. Pick one spot in the garden, keep him on a lead and only stay out for about one to three minutes. If he goes, name it and play with him, or give him a little freedom in the house or garden. If he doesn't go, he should be crated or kept with you, and you should try again in 10 or 20 minutes.

If you allow him to roam in the garden on his own, the chances are that he will have so much fun that he will forget to go and end up coming inside and having an accident on the floor. As your puppy gets to be between 12 and 16 weeks old, you'll find that he can go longer between potty trips. Use your chart to decide how long that should be.

Keeping a chart will track your puppy's progress, but it will also help family members know when to supervise closely and when to allow freedom. If the person who is next in charge of walking the puppy checks the chart, she will know to take the puppy out more frequently and watch him closely for signs that he needs to go.

You can also keep track on your chart of when your puppy has accidents, so that you will know when you need to add in an extra walk or supervise more carefully. Over several weeks of making charts, you will be able to put the charts together and determine whether you are making progress in the right direction, and if you aren't, what you need to do to get back on the right track.

No Papers Please

Using newspapers or potty pads to housetrain your puppy is the surest way to make him unreliable with housetraining. Dogs that are trained to 'go' on newspaper or potty pads never learn to hold it because they go whenever they have to. If you want to housetrain your dog reliably, don't use paper to train him. Take him outside from day one, and don't look back. If you are currently using newspaper, pick it up and throw it away: start taking your dog outside today.

> Using paper in the house gives your dog the impression that there is a safe place to go inside. When the paper is gone, you will have to walk him more frequently and supervise him more carefully, but he will get the idea over time that the only place he can go is outside.

Some people who have dogs weighing less than 2.3kg (5lb) as adults choose to teach their dogs to go in a litter box rather than taking them outside. This may be a desirable option for you if you live in a high-rise flat and it is a long trip to the great outdoors. Using a litter box works on the same principles of paper training, except that the actual potty spot is unique and in no way resembles a carpet or any other surface you are likely to have in your house. It would be ideal to keep this litter box on a balcony or sun porch and walk your dog as though he were going outside to do his business. If you leave the litter box indoors and allow your dog free access to it, you will have the same problems as with dogs that are paper-trained. If your dog can go whenever he wants, he will never learn to hold it and will probably never be truly housetrained.

Using a Lead for Toilet Training

Unless your dog is a rescue dog adopted from a shelter as an adult and absolutely will not go on a leash, it is a good idea to use a lead to take your dog to the toilet training spot. The lead should be about 2m (6ft) long and you should stand in one spot; don't follow the dog all over the garden. Let the dog sniff in a circle around you and really praise him if he goes. Try not to get him into the habit of walking through the neighbourhood unless you want to have to do that in freezing cold weather or pouring rain.

The trick to walking your dog on a lead is to get him to go to the toilet quickly without too much distraction so that, regardless of the weather, your dog will perform his duties quickly and on demand. The lead acts as a way for you to communicate to your dog that you are not outside to play, but to take care of the business at hand.

A good rule of thumb for toilet training for unhousetrained dogs is to only stay out for one to two minutes, no more. If he goes, praise and give freedom. If he doesn't go, either confine him to a crate or gated area, or keep him with you for 20 minutes or so and try again. The message to the dog is, 'If you go, you get freedom; if you don't, you don't.'

Name It, Especially for Rainy or Snowy Days

Dogs that are taught to urinate and defecate on cue are a pleasure to walk. Even in bad weather they go out and do their business, and their owners don't freeze to death waiting for them. Putting the act of going to the toilet on a cue by calling it something will help speed up the whole ordeal. The common names for potty behaviour are Go, Hurry Up or Get Busy.

Through training, you can name each function and your dog will go on command whenever you ask. This is really convenient if you're about to take him inside a shop, a friend's house or the hospital you may visit as a therapy dog team. Because you know they've gone and will last until you leave, you can relax and enjoy your visit. You can name the toilet training by saying whatever your command is going to be as your dog is in the process of going. You can even click and treat as he is going, to give him the idea that doing his business outside is a good thing. It takes a lot of repetitions for the dog to understand that the command means 'go', so be patient and make sure everyone in the family knows exactly what commands are being used.

Make a Toilet Training Spot in Your Garden

You may also want to consider creating a toilet training spot in your garden, a designated place where your dog can do his business without interfering with the beauty of the rest of the garden. Creating one area that clearly says 'toilet' to your dog will not only help you housetrain him, but it will also keep him from using the whole garden as his toilet. That way, if you like to have barbecues, or you have children who play in the garden, you won't have to worry about scooping the whole area.

To build the toilet training spot, you'll want to use materials that offer good drainage and the ability to disinfect. Here are some training spot recommendations:

- Make a square or rectangular box out of garden timbers cut to the dimensions you wish. Large dogs probably need a 2.4 x 2.4m (8x 8ft) area; smaller dogs could probably live with a 1.2 x 1.2m (4x 4ft) space.
- Cover the bottom with several bags of sand.
- Cover the sand with a variety of sizes of crushed stone. Some people prefer the tiny size often called 'pea stone'; others prefer the 25mm (1in) diameter type.

Designated training spots will allow you to scoop easily and disinfect with a bleach solution regularly. A weed sprayer with a 30:70 solution of bleach and water works well as a disinfectant. Even in tight quarters, this arrangement eliminates excessive odour and unsanitary conditions. A metal rake may also help you to redistribute the stone and sand.

Confinement Works

Young puppies, or even adult dogs, that are not housetrained should not have free access to the house. If you allow too much freedom too soon, you will create housetraining problems. Dogs often consider where they eat and sleep their home, and the rest of the house the outside. That is why a puppy kept in the kitchen will often run to the dining room and do his business if he gets loose. Using a crate to keep your puppy confined when you cannot watch him is an excellent housetraining tool.

The confinement area should be relatively small, to keep the puppy from designating one end for sleeping and the other for the toilet.

Try not to put any cozy blankets, newspaper or bedding inside until he has proven himself by staying dry in the crate for two weeks in a row. For dogs that cannot be crate-trained for some reason, confinement by means of baby gates is a good idea. If the dog is walked on a regular basis, he will do his best to keep his gated area clean.

Control the Food and Water

A puppy is like a sieve: what goes in will come out. Pay attention to how much and how often he eats and drinks, and regulate what goes in so you can regulate what comes out. Your unhousetrained dog should not have free access to food and water, because he will eat and drink whenever he wants and you will be less able to predict when he'll need to go out. In order to housetrain a dog, you need to stick to a strict food and water schedule and make sure that he is walked at regular intervals. Puppies that have a regular feeding routine are easy to predict; if you feed and water them on a regular schedule, they will go out on schedule.

The best way to help a puppy develop a reliable housetraining schedule is to feed roughly at the same time each day and not leave water out all day and night. Put the food down for 10 minutes; pick it up if he doesn't finish and put it away until the next meal. Feed a young puppy of 7–12 weeks old three times a day; feed an older puppy or adult dog twice a day. Put the water down at regular intervals and pay attention to how much he drinks. Remember: what goes in comes out.

Don't Punish Your Puppy for Mistakes

An important aspect of housetraining a dog successfully is to reward success rather than punish mistakes. Mistakes are really your fault for not walking your puppy at the right time. If you'd like to hit yourself over the head with a rolled-up newspaper, feel free! Your puppy will not learn not to go in the house by being scolded or punished. What he will learn is to avoid going in front of you and instead go under the dining-room table when no one is looking. The end result is that it will be nearly impossible to get him to go on a lead, because he will come to believe that going in front of someone is wrong.

Providing a consequence for unproductive trips to the toilet spot is a good idea. The most logical consequence is a lack of freedom. A dog that normally goes at a certain hour, such as first thing in the morning or last thing at night, should not be allowed to play freely in the house or garden until he has had a productive trip outside.

Deal with mistakes by ignoring the puppy for a while. Put him in a crate or gated room, clean up the mess and make a note of the time of the accident. Keep track of your dog's mistakes to see whether there is any pattern to them and whether you should add in extra walks.

Proper Clean-up Procedures for Accidents

When your puppy has an accident on the carpet or floor, it is essential to clean it up as quickly and as thoroughly as possible to eliminate any lingering odours, because any remaining smell will draw the puppy back to that spot. Here are some tips for cleaning up urine on carpet:

1. Blot as much as possible with paper towels.
2. Pour a 250ml (8fl oz) glass of water over the spot to dilute the urine.
3. Blot with more paper towels until there is not even a hint of yellow on the towels.

4. Spray carpet cleaner over the entire spot, and scrub it with a brush or a sponge.
5. Spray the area again and follow the product directions for standing time and vacuuming. (Repeat as needed.)
6. Spray with an enzyme inhibitor, such as Febreze, which eliminates the odour, following the product directions exactly.

If you are not sure you know about all the spots where your dog has gone, consider purchasing a black light (available in some dog supply catalogues) to detect urine stains on carpet.

Cleaning up urine or faeces on hardwood floors should be done a little differently to prevent permanent damage to the floor.

1. Wipe up excess with paper towels.
2. Mix up a bucket of Flash or similar floor cleaner and water, and wash the area thoroughly with a mop or sponge.
3. Dry the area thoroughly with a rag or paper towels.
4. Spray an enzyme inhibitor (made especially for this purpose) on a cloth, and wipe down the area one last time.

Cleaning up faeces on carpet can be tricky. Make sure you remove as much as possible with paper towels before treating the area, to avoid rubbing the excess into the carpet and thus compounding the problem.

1. Remove all solid waste with paper towels.
2. Spray with carpet cleaner and rub out as much as possible with a sponge.
3. Spray the area again and use a scrubbing brush to deep-clean the fibres of the carpet.
4. Spray the area with carpet cleaner again and follow the product directions for standing time and vacuuming. (Repeat as needed.)
5. Spray with enzyme inhibitor (available in most pet shops) to permanently eliminate the odour.

6. If your dog tends to continue to go back to the same spot over and over again, consider rearranging the furniture a bit to block access to that spot.

Cleaning any area where an accident occurred is essential to keeping your dog on track with his housetraining. If you are cleaning up more than a couple of accidents a week, you are probably not walking your puppy outside often enough or are allowing too much freedom too soon. Remember that limiting a puppy's freedom is half the key to housetraining and is only temporary until your puppy proves he knows where to 'go' and is completely reliable.

Cleaning up accidents efficiently is very important. A dog's sense of smell is intense; if accidents are not cleaned up thoroughly, the odour can draw the animal back to that spot time and again. Many products on the market today help not only to clean up the mess but also to neutralize the odour, making it less likely that your dog will be drawn back to the same spot; one such, Febreze, is available from most supermarkets.

Dogs need to go out at least once during a four-hour period if confined to a small area, such as a crate. If they have more freedom or free access to food and water, they may have to go more frequently. Most adult, housetrained dogs need to be walked first thing in the morning, sometime around midday, after work and before bed. A midday visit from a pet sitter can help your adult dog maintain housetraining manners.

A lack of housetraining is a silly reason to give up a dog to a shelter, but living with a dog that uses your house as his toilet is no picnic either. Housetraining manners are the most basic of training issues that must be accomplished if a dog is going to live peaceably with humans. The tricks to housetraining come down to some very basic elements: confine the dog in some way, put him on a schedule and keep track of his successes and failures, control the food and water bowls, walk him outdoors in short, frequent spurts and avoid punishing mistakes. If you follow these guidelines, your dog should be making fairly good progress within a month or six weeks' time.

Shetland Sheepdog sitting

Occasionally a dog may have a medical problem that is interfering with housetraining. If you were making good progress with housetraining but your dog suddenly regresses, consider getting your vet to check a urine and stool sample for signs of infection or parasites. Both of these medical conditions can easily be treated with medication, and will often present themselves as a regression in a housetraining programme.

It is silly to pursue an issue behaviourally if the real problem lies in a medical condition. If, despite your best efforts, you find your dog's housetraining problems baffling, or you adopted your dog late in his life and he came with a host of serious behaviour problems, you may want to consider the help of a professional dog trainer or behaviourist.

CHAPTER 15

Pulling on the Lead

I f there is a common problem among dogs, it is pulling on the lead to get where they want to go. From the biggest Great Dane to the tiniest Chihuahua, all dogs, regardless of their size, learn to pull on their leads from an early age.

The Only Solution Is Training

Lead pulling doesn't seem to be such a big problem until you try to walk around the block with a dog that thinks he's the lead dog in a sled team, determined to reach the park in record time. Pulling on the lead is one of the major reasons people stop taking their dogs for walks – it takes all the fun out of a leisurely walk around the neighbourhood when one of your arms feels as though it is being pulled out of its socket.

Why do dogs pull?
Dogs pull because it gets them where they want to go. If every time your dog leaves the house he is allowed to tug at the end of the lead and you follow him wherever he pulls you, you are reinforcing the behaviour and letting your dog think it is OK.

If you look in pet stores and in pet supply catalogues, you will see dozens of devices that supposedly magically stop your dog from pulling. The truth of the matter, however, is that dogs will continue to pull until you teach them to stop, regardless of the equipment you are using. Only you, as your dog's trusted companion, can choose what method you want to use to teach your dog to walk with you instead of drag you, and there are many options out there that you can try. The key to any training programme, however, is *you* – how much time you invest in the project, and how consistent you are about sticking to it until the job is done.

Define Your Terms

Whenever you want to cure any behaviour problem, it is a good idea to sit down and work out what you would like your dog to do instead. In this case, it is important to define how you want your dog to behave on the lead. Do you want him to walk at perfect heel position, or is a loose lead sufficient? Where exactly would you like your dog to be, and what will it look like when he's there? Will your arm be relaxed or extended, is sniffing OK, and which side should he be on?

Narrowing down what you are looking for gives you a better idea of what you are going to reinforce, and will help you recognize it and reward it. Only by reinforcing the right behaviour will you be able to get rid of the undesirable one. If you don't know what your dog has to do to get the reward, you will not be successful at getting rid of pulling and teaching him an acceptable alternative. Sit down with your family now and decide how you want your dog to behave on the lead.

A good barometer for heeling is to pay attention to the slack in the lead. Look at the arm that is holding the lead: if your elbow has a bend in it, the dog is walking with you nicely; if your arm is straight, you've got some training to do.

Lack of Exercise Contribution

Nowhere is a lack of exercise more apparent than when a dog is on the lead. A dog with few outlets for his energy will pull, spin and tug on the lead to get where he wants to go. Giving your dog appropriate outlets for his energy, such as playing with other dogs, swimming and playing fetch, will help give you a more calm on-lead companion. Active dogs need at least 30 minutes to an hour a day of flat-out running to take the edge off their energy. Without this outlet, you can expect behaviour problems.

Exercise is part of a dog's basic needs for mental, physical and emotional stability, and to ignore this fact is to set your dog up for failure. If you don't have the time to exercise your dog to the point of fatigue, consider hiring a pet sitter, dog walker or day care kennels to help you give your dog the exercise he needs. Trying to train a dog that is not getting enough exercise is a project in frustration and should be avoided at all costs.

Walk Without Pulling

Teaching your dog to walk at your side, rather than pull your arm off, requires lots of practice and repetition. This is not behaviour that is going to change overnight. Remember that pulling works, or has worked, for quite a long time for most dogs, and behaviour that isn't corrected is repeated. A huge step in the right direction is to stop following the dog when the lead is tight and he's pulling you. This may mean suspending all walks around the block so that he doesn't have the opportunity to practise pulling.

Managing your dog's behaviour by not allowing him to practise it isn't teaching him to walk next to you, but it's a step in the right direction, since he isn't being reprimanded for the wrong behaviour. Following are some tips for teaching loose-lead walking:

· Walk at a brisk pace and change direction frequently so that your dog has to pay attention to where you are going. The more turns you offer, the more your dog has to pay attention to where you are.

· Once you get the hang of walking and turning frequently, start to pay attention to the moment your dog turns to follow you, and click and treat him for catching up to you.

· At first, you may want to stop walking for a moment after the click so that the dog realizes what exactly he's getting clicked for. Use really delicious treats that your dog loves to keep his attention focused on you.

· Start off practising in a distraction-free place, and gradually go to busier places when your dog starts to understand what you want.

· Attaching a 2m (6ft) lead to your waist will keep your hands free for this exercise, so you will be able to click and treat your dog when he is next to you. Remember that the message you are sending to your dog is that pulling does not get him where he wants to go, because when he pulls in one direction, it makes you go the other way.

· For most dogs, the faster you walk the better, since a steady pace forces them to pay attention to where you are going next.

· Using a clicker to mark the action of being next to you will shorten your training time by half. The clicker tells the dog exactly what he's doing right to earn the reward. The clicker is clearer and more precise than any other tool you can use.

When you want to change behaviour that has been working for the dog for quite some time, you need to reinforce the right behaviour often and with a high-value reward. Your dog has been pulling to get where he's going for as long as you've had him, so in order to get rid of pulling, you must replace it with something he finds more rewarding. In order for him to choose to walk next to you over pulling, you will have to do lots of repetitions with tasty rewards.

 Remember that you are building your dog's training history for loose-lead walking. If you are going to do this effectively, both the rate of and value of his rewards have to be high.

Really great bribes can take the shape of treats such as cheese, freeze-dried liver, roast beef or chicken, or favourite games such as tug or fetch. Whatever the reward, the dog has to want it more than he wants to pull you. Be creative and fun, and your dog will soon be trotting happily next to you.

Adding Duration to Your Walks

From a training standpoint, duration refers to the amount of time your dog can maintain the requested behaviour. In this case, it's the length of time that the dog has to be next to you in order to earn his click and treat. Once your dog starts to catch on to getting clicked for coming back to your side, you can then raise the criteria to his coming back to your side and staying there for a step or two. Eventually, you will build the length of time the dog must walk next to you to several minutes, until the dog no longer wants to pull. Remember, duration refers to the length of time the dog must perform the action before he gets rewarded. Practise getting him to walk with you for different lengths of time around a variety of distractions until he can trot happily next to you under any circumstance.

Changing the Variables and Distractions

Practising in a new environment – with people, dogs, cars, bicycles and other distractions – is critical to the reliability of the training. Changing too many of these variables at once, however, will make your dog's walking next to you fall apart. To help your dog to learn to stay with you despite the distractions, change one variable at a time. The variables involved in heeling refer to how close or far you are to the distractions and how intense the distractions are (one person, a crowd, children, adults, people with dogs, wildlife, cars, bikes and so forth).

By controlling the variables and working slowly to introduce distractions while you maintain your dog's ability to walk at heel, you will teach your dog to walk nicely on a lead, regardless of the distractions in the environment. Don't ever be afraid to stop the training session and make it easier for the dog to be right if things are going badly and your dog could use some extra help.

The length of time you choose should be random so that your dog does not pick up on a pattern. It is probably best not to increase the length of time all at once, but instead to start with low numbers and then gradually increase the time as the dog catches on to the game.

Controlling Heeling

There are two major variables involved in teaching your dog to heel: the distance to the distraction and the intensity of the distraction. The distance between your dog and the distraction is too close if you can't get the dog to work properly. If this is the case, you should back away from the action to a point where your dog will perform the training well. Once your dog is working well, you can decrease the distance between your dog and the distraction, bringing him closer to the action when you are sure your dog can handle it.

Setting your dog up for success is the key to becoming a good dog trainer. Here are some ways that you can set your dog up for success.

· Reduce the intensity of the distraction (quieter, slower, less of it, for example) as needed.
· Use your best treats; training is difficult, so make it worth his while.
· Offer a high rate of reinforcement in a new environment.
· Slow the rate down (click and treat less frequently) for longer versions of the training (dog stays with you longer), and when the dog starts to be able to perform the training reliably.

Choose what distraction you will start with, and set it up so that your dog can be successful. The intensity of the distraction has to do with its speed, noise level and quantity. The intensity is too high when your dog can't perform the training because he is too distracted. The solution to this problem is to tone down the distraction by making it go slower and quieter, or having less of it.

Common Distractions

Another consideration when you are working your dog around distractions is the type of distraction you are working on. There are three major categories of distractions: things that move, things that smell, and things that make noise.

1. **Things that move.** This category incites your dog's prey drive, his desire to chase after things that move. Every dog has a different level of distractibility, but most dogs find things that move irresistible. Examples include cars, bikes, squirrels, runners, other dogs, motorcycles, balls and children.
2. **Things that smell.** The majority of dogs are motivated most by their stomachs, so, for the hunting breeds especially, 'nose to the ground' behaviour can be quite a challenge. Examples are food, animals, other animals' faeces and wildlife.
3. **Things that make noise.** Some dogs are more sensitive to sound than others. The average dog that is simply curious will get over it quickly and learn to ignore sounds if you change the variables, distance and intensity slowly.

Always be sure there isn't a physical reason why your dog won't walk with you. Check his feet for cuts, make sure the pavement isn't too hot or that his feet aren't stinging from salt-treated roads in the wintertime.

Distractions need to be worked into the training gradually. If distractions are too frequent or intense, the dog will get overexcited and be unable to concentrate, and no real learning will occur. It is important that you pay attention to his excitement level and tone down the distractions so that he is able to absorb the lesson.

The Mule Impersonator

Nervous dogs often plant their rears and will not move forward. They will not move or follow you with any amount of coaxing or cooing. There are several tricks you can use to get these dogs to follow you:

1. Put tension in the lead, but don't pull. Make sure the lead is hooked to a regular collar, not a training collar.
2. As soon as your dog takes a step towards you to steady himself, be ready to click and treat and lavish with praise (some dogs take a while, so be patient).
3. Repeat this every time your dog stops. Don't go back to him; simply ignore the wrong behaviour and pay attention to the right one.
4. Within 10 minutes or so, most dogs give up their stubborn mule impression and go with you. Some dogs may need you to do this over several sessions before they give up.

Use Grand Rewards

Teaching your dog to heel can be time-consuming and boring – for both of you – if you don't come up with ideas to make it more interesting and fun. One way to make things more fun is to hide the rewards around your training area before you start your session. It will be such a surprise to the dog to be rewarded with a delicious treat or a great toy that he wasn't expecting to be pulled out of the bushes. The element of surprise will make you far more interesting to your dog, and it will make your dog much more willing to learn to walk with you.

Can nervous dogs learn to ignore new sounds and walk at heel?
You can train any dog to walk at heel. For the nervous dog, it would be best to teach him to deal with novel noises and build his confidence first. Once he loses his skittishness, you can then try to teach him to walk to heel around such distractions.

You may also want to consider using a variety of rewards paired with the click. Some examples are a game of tug, a game of fetch, a stuffed toy, a fantastic belly or flank rub, and lots of excited praise. You can teach your dog that you are interesting and full of great surprises by hiding your goodies everywhere and keeping your dog guessing about what you're going to pull out next.

Training Equipment

Training collars, head halters and other devices are just that: devices. Their purpose is to manage pulling while you are teaching your dog to heel. The aim should be to have your dog learn to walk to heel with the help of a training device, and then to wean the dog off that device and get them to walk to heel without it.

Collars and Leads

You can find several training devices that keep dogs from pulling. The most common are the regular slip collar or choke chain, the pinch collar and the head halter. The slip collar works by restricting the dog's airway for a fraction of a second and making it unpleasant for him to pull. The pinch collar works by pinching the skin around the dog's neck and making it unpleasant to pull. The head halter works by pulling the dog's head down, making it impossible to walk until the dog stops pulling and walks closer to the handler.

As with any device, you must teach your dog the step-by-step process for heeling, and in most cases this should occur before you start using the device itself. After the dog has learned how to get rewarded, the use of a training device will help you sort out the various distractions. Special situations, such as the veterinary clinic, may require extra management before your dog is completely trained. No one device is right for every dog, but the head halter is probably the most useful for most dogs.

No device will 'teach' your dog to walk to heel. You are the one that must break down this lead-walking issue into simple steps that you can incorporate into training a little at a time. The training devices will help you manage behaviour, but that is all.

Head-Halter Benefits

There is one particular name brand of head halter, the Halti head collar, which tends to fit better than most of the others available on the market today. It has two adjustable straps: one for the neck and one for the muzzle. The lead clips underneath the dog's chin. Think of the way a halter on a horse fits, and you'll have an idea of how this works. The principle behind why the head halter is superior to other training devices is that it controls the dog's forward movement by controlling the dog's head. You would never expect to move a horse by pulling on its neck, for instance, but you can easily move such a large animal in the direction you want to go by guiding it by its head – well, at least most of the time!

This same principle works for dogs. The head halter is not a muzzle – the dog can still eat, catch a ball and bite with it on, and no dog should be left unattended while wearing it. If your dog should try to bite or eat something he shouldn't while wearing the head halter, you can easily close his mouth by gently pulling on the lead. The pressure that exerts will easily close his mouth and pull his head down, effectively preventing him from continuing what he had been doing. The head halter is sometimes described as self-correcting, meaning the handler does not

Hound Cross wearing a head halter

have to pull on the lead or yank the dog in any way to get him to stop what he is doing. It is also important to note that if you choose to use this device, you should attach only a 2m (6ft) lead to it, never an extendable or retractable one. If your dog were to take off after something and hit the end of a long lead while wearing a head halter, he could injure his neck. Introduce the head halter over a period of about two weeks. The longer you take to make this fun for the dog, the more useful a training tool it will be.

The introduction of the head halter should be a gradual process, where you slowly teach the dog that wearing it is fun and means good stuff is about to happen. Your aim is to make him as excited to see the head halter as he is to see his lead. Using a clicker and the tastiest treats, introduce the head halter by following these steps:

1. Show the halter to your dog and click and treat him for sniffing at it.
2. Open the nose loop, and click and treat your dog for poking his nose through it to get at the treat.
3. Once he's eagerly putting her nose through the loop on his own, give him a good-sized treat, and while he's chewing, fasten the neck strap.
4. Let him move around a bit, and click and treat him for not pawing at his nose.
5. If your dog gets the nose loop off, take the whole thing off and leave him alone for 10 minutes or so. Completely ignoring him will make him all the more eager to work with you again. The idea here is that he will want to keep the halter on, because you pay extra attention to him and give special treats only when he has it on.

6. Later, when he isn't pawing as much, attach a lead to the clip under the chin and repeat steps 4 and 5. You will have to go back and click and treat him for walking without pawing at his face every time you introduce a new distraction or variable.

7. You are now ready to use the head halter on your walks, but go slowly. Take your dog for a short walk, and click and treat him for walking outside without pawing at his face. Keep the walk to no more than five minutes long.

8. As your dog gets used to wearing the head halter in public, you can gradually increase the distractions, the length of time you walk him, and any of the other variables.

Remember to make it easy for the dog to be right if you notice any regression around distractions. This is especially common when other dogs are present. The head halter can be a wonderful tool for helping you manage your dog around distractions and teaching him not to pull, but introducing it takes time, so don't rush your dog.

> Think of the head halter as a guide. Use it to guide your dog on his walks. Never pull, snap or correct your dog in the halter, as it could damage his neck or spine.

If this device isn't useful for a dog, it is usually because the owner rushed the introduction because the dog seemed to tolerate it fairly well. Don't be fooled – just as with training other things, you get out what you put in. The following are tips for making this work for you.

· Be patient during this introduction. The head halter is a more useful tool if you introduce it slowly and let the dog learn to like wearing it (up to a week or two).

· You will have no need for jerks or corrections with a head halter; in fact, doing so can injure a dog's neck or spine.

· Make sure you read the halter's directions carefully before you use it on your dog. It's important that you teach your dog to wear it and avoid letting him lunge or pull while wearing it.
· Lunging or pulling can injure your dog's neck or spine, causing him discomfort and long-term medical problems.
· If you have trouble, find a qualified positive trainer to help you introduce this piece of equipment to your dog.

Teaching your dog to walk without pulling is a time-consuming task, but it is well worth the effort. Having a dog that will walk politely beside you without yanking your arm off makes him a more pleasant companion that you won't mind taking anywhere with you. Remember that you need to build your dog's saving account for not pulling through lots of practice and consistency. At the very least, stop letting him practise pulling by stopping every time he tugs at the end of the lead. By using the right equipment, introducing distractions slowly and controlling the distance, you will gradually teach your canine companion that walking with you, rather than dragging you, is the better alternative.

CHAPTER 16

Running Away

Dogs that don't come when they are called have learned that getting away from you is rewarding. If they run off and find things to eat, roll in and play with, then running away has huge benefits and it doesn't give them much incentive to come and be with you.

Why Do Dogs Run Away?

When the average person calls her dog, she puts the lead back on and goes home, or puts the dog in a crate and goes to work or puts the dog in the car and drives away. Since it normally isn't beneficial for the dog to come to his owner, because his owner doesn't provide a very rewarding consequence, the dog chooses to reward himself instead, and runs away.

The difference between a trained dog that comes when called and an untrained dog that doesn't is based on the dog's perception of who controls what he wants. Dogs behave in ways that benefit them, so the key to having a dog that is always willing to come when called is making it worth the dog's while, regardless of the distraction. Trained dogs know that their owners hold the keys to everything they want, and the rule is that the dog must do something to get it.

Use a Lead to Control the Variable Training

The most important thing to remember is that every time your dog takes off and has a good time, it is harder for you to reinforce the training. Don't allow an untrained dog off the lead in an unsafe area or an area where he will be difficult to catch. A dog that has an unreliable recall is a danger to himself. He doesn't have good judgment, and will often run into the road, get lost or eat something harmful. If you love your dog, use a lead in unfenced areas so that you do not give your dog the opportunity to run away.

When you use a lead to teach your dog to come, you are using it to limit his options. The fewer options he has, the more likely he is to choose coming to you on command over running in the opposite direction.

Keeping your dog on a lead gives him the ability to be right more often and allows you to reinforce those choices, making it likely he will choose to listen to you again and again. When you eventually get to the point where you are not using a lead, it will be easy to get rid of it and still have the same level of behaviour. Since you have not used the lead to teach him to come by tugging on it, but instead used it merely to limit his options, you have made it more likely that he will choose you over the distraction.

Make Sure the Rewards Are Worth the Effort

Your dog needs you to use the best possible rewards if he's going to choose coming to you over pursuing a distraction. Remember that a squirrel, cat, child or another dog is a thrill to chase, bark at or sniff around. If your dog chooses to be with you as against the distraction, make sure you have the best treats, toys or games as the reward. You will mark your dog's action of turning in your direction with a click and follow it by a treat, a game or an opportunity to interact with the distraction (but only after checking with you first). Using rewards in this way is not a bribe; you are simply making sure that your dog checks with you before he gets what he wants. For dogs that learn this game, it almost completely eliminates the desire to run away. Using rewards in this way means that you control the dog's access to what he wants, and you pay up when he checks with you.

How can I speed up my dog's response to Come?
Using a reward that your dog really likes can make the difficult task of coming when called more fun and rewarding for the dog. Experiment with different types of food, toys, games and opportunities, and see how it affects your dog's performance.

Ideas for Rewards

Making the rewards variable and exciting will enhance your dog's performance and make the process of teaching your dog to come all the more fun. Here are some things to keep in mind when you are considering different types of rewards in your training programme.

- Food rewards can include cheese, liver, chicken, beef, tortellini, sausages, roast beef and steak.
- Toy rewards can include stuffed toys, balls, tug toys, Frisbees, etc.
- Games rewards, such as fetch, tug and Frisbee, can help a high-energy dog stay focused on you and redirect the energy that would have been used to chase the distraction.
- Real-life rewards include the opportunity to chase the distraction (a ball, a squirrel, a leaf), to say hello to the person or other dog, to play with the group of dogs off the lead nearby, to swim in the pond, romp through the snow, roll in the smell or whatever.

The best way to use a non-food reward is to limit the time you interact with the dog after the click to a few seconds if it's a game, or to use the real-life reward at the end of the session as a way to remind the dog that coming to you is just the most terrific thing ever.

Leadership Matters

Ninety per cent of a dog's recall has to do with who's in charge. Dogs with firm, strong leaders almost always come when called, because you are in charge of everything great and your judgment is worth trusting. Being a leader in no way implies being a bully or making your dog do something; in fact, true leaders never have to force a dog to do anything. Leadership is about setting limits and having rules about what is allowed and what is not allowed. Having guidelines is essential if your dog is going to do as you wish.

Quite simply, a strong leader controls resources that the dog wants access to, including his dinner, the outdoors, attention and affection, and space (including sleeping places). In a nutshell, leadership entails being first, being more powerful and being in charge. Your ideas and decisions rule, not the dog's.

Being the leader means that you control the resources that the dog wants. It does not mean, under any circumstances, that you dominate or bully the dog in any way. Here are some guidelines for you to review:

1. Nothing in life is free. Your dog must do something to get something.
2. Respond quickly to commands. Pick a number of seconds that you'll give your dog to respond to the command; if he doesn't respond on the first command within the time frame you've chosen, he doesn't get whatever you were about to give him.
3. No dogs on your bed. No dog, let alone a dog with a behaviour problem (especially a recall problem), should be allowed to sleep on the highest, most privileged spot in the house: your bed.
4. Leaders go first through doorways and up and down stairs. Teach your dog to wait and let you go first.
5. No dogs on the furniture; your dog should be on the floor or in his crate or bed.
6. Leaders control space and move about without interference. Don't step over or around your dog; if he's in your way, make him move.
7. Leaders initiate attention and games. Pushy dogs that hound you with toys or nudging should be ignored until they give up. You can call them to you later when it's your idea to play.

When you require your dog to earn privileges, you are in charge. When the dog gets them for free, he doesn't need you and won't trust your judgment. Controlling whatever it is that the dog wants is the key to controlling the dog's behaviour.

You, as the leader, can control what your dog wants by controlling his options and what he's allowed to have. The rule is that when you are experiencing behaviour problems, you need to be strict about allowing privileges and having house rules. When your dog behaves in a more acceptable way in a few months' time, you can relax some of the rules here and there without losing your status as leader. Think of it as similar to allowing a child to stay up later in the summertime. Staying up later in the summer is a special thing for a child; once September comes, she knows she will have to go to bed at the usual time.

> If you are strict at first, you can relax your rules later and allow your dog privileges without losing ground. Having rules is essential for a dog that is content and relaxed. Just like children, dogs take comfort in the fact that someone else is in charge so that they can enjoy just being dogs.

Building a Foundation for Come

The foundation for Come is the most important part of the exercise. It requires your dog to turn away from the distraction and look back at you (and eventually to move towards you as well). The Come command is really a Leave It command, because the dog has to turn away from what he wants and come back to you. The more reliable your dog is about turning away from the things he wants, the more able you will be to get him to come to you at any time, and in any situation. If you teach a strong foundation for self-control (see Chapter 9), Come will be easier to train, and your dog will be reliable anywhere you take him. Although you have already taught Come to your dog (see Chapter 5), take a moment to review the shaping steps again:

1. Stand with your dog on the lead and don't let him get to what he wants; when your dog turns away from what he wants and looks back at you, click and treat.
2. If it takes your dog more than a minute to look back, you are too close to the distraction; go back away from it.
3. When the dog is turning in your direction easily, run backwards as he turns to look at you and let him catch you. Click your dog as he is moving towards you and put the treat at your feet.
4. Practise putting the treat between your feet, so when he takes it, it will be easier for you to catch him.

5. Practise handling your dog's collar and leading him by it, clicking and treating him for tolerating being led by it.
6. Name the command Come when you have the dog by the collar.
7. Change the environment and distractions; practise in various places.
8. Use a longer lead – 4–8m (12–25ft) – and repeat the exercise from the beginning.
9. Let your lead drag until your dog proves that he understands the command Come.
10. Vary the size and type of rewards to keep the dog guessing as to what he'll get as a reward.

Change Old Patterns

Old habits die hard, and a dog that consistently runs away to entertain himself is practising the very opposite of the behaviour you are trying to teach him. If your dog has run away a lot in the past and got away with rewarding himself again and again, you are going to have to put in a lot of time to prevent him from running away, and to reward him for coming with really memorable rewards.

Don't miss opportunities to reward your dog for good behaviour. Even if you are not directly training your dog to Come, reward him for any amount of checking with you. This, in and of itself, sometimes is enough to get the checking behaviour started.

Some dogs refuse to come to you because nothing good happens when they do. For instance, just before you leave for work, you call your dog in from the garden put him in his crate and leave him there for eight hours. Or at the park, you call him away from his dog friends and then put him in the car and go straight home. Try to change this situation by calling him several times before you actually need to leave, and allow him to go back to playing as the reward. Changing *your* pattern of behaviour (calling the dog and putting him back on the lead, for instance) may be harder than you think.

Miniature Pinscher coming out of her crate

Again, having a plan of action – what you desire and what you will reward – will make training easier. Prepare ahead of time how you are going to react, and you will be rewarded by a dog that is much more likely to come to you than run away and reward himself.

Keep Recall Positive

Punishment only stops undesirable behaviour – it doesn't teach the dog anything. By the time you've punished your dog for running away, you have him back. In his mind, you are punishing him for coming to you, making it far less likely that you'll be able to get him to respond enthusiastically in the future.

Remote punishment through the use of electronic collars is also not appropriate in the hands of the average pet owner. Even when used by professionals, such devices can teach the dog to be distrustful and fearful of his environment. It is much safer and more reasonable to teach your dog what you expect of him and avoid punishment altogether. When it comes down to it, punishment misses the point; it is almost always issued too late to be instructive, and if it isn't delivered with perfect timing, it will have absolutely no positive effect on the dog's behaviour. Use your time and energy wisely – teach the dog what is expected of him, instead of punishing him for making a mistake.

Teaching your dog that the consequences for coming when called are good is the best way to have a reliable recall. A good consequence could be a few minutes of attention and affection from you, a really good treat or game, or the opportunity to go straight back to what you called him away from.

The Importance of Exercise

The more exercise your dog gets, the more likely he will be to come back when you call him. A dog with no opportunity to run and explore will be less likely to return to you on demand. Make sure your dog gets to play and run for at least 30 minutes to an hour (or longer!) every day. Ideally, he should exercise and wrestle with other dogs; if interactive play isn't possible, chasing a ball, swimming or other energy-expending pursuits are essential.

If there is an easy way to boost the solving of a behaviour problem, this is it. Almost any professional dog trainer will tell you that a tired dog is a good dog! Confinement in a garden or yard doesn't count. Most dogs don't want to be by themselves, and without a companion they will often bark, howl, chew and escape the confines of the garden. Meaningful interaction is the key to engaging the dog's mind and body and making sure that his needs for exercise are met.

Play hide-and-seek with your whole family, and take turns letting the dog find you. Call him back and forth to you in the garden or in a big field or at the beach (get him to drag a long lead if you think he'll take off). Play fetch, blow bubbles for him to chase and catch, or take him swimming. Whatever activities you choose, get out and get active, and enjoy your dog and the great outdoors. I bet you will find that providing more exercise makes your dog more likely to stay closer to you in the great outdoors.

Consider this: the more time *you* spend exercising your dog, the better you'll feel, too! All levels of the relationship between family and pet benefit from the time you spend together.

Safe Confinement

You can confine your dog in any number of ways, but it's important to pay careful attention to details so that he can't escape. Bear in mind that no dog should be left unsupervised outdoors unless you have an absolutely escape-proof fence or wall. You can call a fence company to come and design a dog pen to fit your needs, but dogs that are confined outdoors tend to develop barking problems.

If you build your own pen, you must keep several things in mind during design and construction. Ideally, you should bury 6mm ($1/4$in) mesh wire about 75–100mm (3–4in) under a gravel base; this way, if your dog decides to dig, he can't dig out. Watch your dog carefully to make sure he doesn't eat the gravel. There are several options you can consider for the bottom surface of the pen. A cement slab may be a good choice if there is adequate shade, but it is not the most comfortable surface to lie on in extreme weather conditions (either hot or cold). One very effective solution is concrete patio blocks (or pavers) surrounded by crushed stone. The size of the stone can be whatever you feel would be best for your dog.

Depending on the size of your dog pen, you could put some kind of kennel or shelter at one end, use patio block for half the length, and leave the rest as plain stone. This arrangement makes it easier to disinfect the pen, keeps the smell to a minimum and is attractive to look at. A locked gate is essential to prevent anyone from stealing your dog. It is really not a good idea to leave your dog unattended, but in circumstances where you need to be gone for an extended period, a pen will at least give your dog a chance to relieve himself in an appropriate permitted place.

Invisible Fences

An invisible fence is a buried wire around the perimeter of your property, providing an electrical barrier that prevents your dog from leaving the garden. To keep your dog within the confines of the garden, he wears a collar that makes an electrical correction if it crosses the barrier. The biggest problem with these fences is that they do not prevent people or animals from coming onto your property, which is why you should never leave your dog unsupervised in an invisibly fenced area.

Invisible fencing lets you restrict your dog's access to certain areas, such as swimming pools, driveways or decorative gardens. In order for this kind of fencing to be used humanely, your dog must be taught to respect the barrier. Hire a qualified professional dog trainer to help you teach your dog where the boundaries are and how to avoid being corrected.

There is some controversy regarding invisible fences and the type of correction they give the dog, and whether or not that correction is humane. The bottom line, regardless of opinions, is that you must do what you feel is best for your dog.

Although this book promotes positive training methods, if someone can't afford to put fences around their garden properly, an invisible fence is much better than doing nothing. Not using preventative measures increases the risk of the dog getting lost or killed. Keep in mind that some dogs are not bothered by the electrical correction and will run through it. A physical barrier, in the form of chain link or solid wood, is a better choice for dogs like these.

Front-Door Safety

Making sure your dog doesn't slip out of the front door is essential to keeping him safe. Try to prevent front-door escapes by thinking ahead and perhaps denying access to the door through which your dog is most likely to escape. Tighten a screen door, if you have one, so that it closes more quickly, or put a lockable baby gate in the doorway to prevent escapes.

Teach your children to be aware of where the dog is when they are coming and going. Put your dog in a crate or gated room when there are a lot of people around – family parties and holiday gatherings are notorious times for dogs to escape and be hit by cars. When you have less control of the home environment, pay special attention to your dog's environment; prevention is half the cure.

Your first job is to teach your dog that looking back at you is the best way to gain access to the things he wants. If he has this basic foundation, your chances for a successful recall will be greater.

Spend some time teaching your dog appropriate door manners, such as sitting and staying without going through the door (even if it's wide open) until told to do so. This requires lots of on-lead set-ups with a helper to hold the lead in case your dog tries to make a break. You'll want to practise at first with the door shut and then gradually build up to your dog holding the Stay while you open and close the door. You can even increase the difficulty by actually going through the door and leaving the dog in Stay. The key point to remember here is to reward the dog for holding the Stay, not coming through the door. Make sure you practise regularly, and provide a high rate of reward for the right behaviour.

Teaching your dog reliable recall is likely to be a more complicated task than you ever imagined. It is not just a training issue, but a relationship and management issue as well. Teaching a strong foundation for Come is essential to getting your dog to realize that you are worth paying attention to, even in a new environment. Once you have accomplished this reliably, your job will then be to change the behaviour and get your dog to perform the basic task of looking back at you around all different kinds of distractions. In addition to investing the time it will take to teach your dog a reliable recall, take the steps necessary to create a safe and limited environment that he can enjoy.

CHAPTER 17

Jumping on People

A common behaviour problem that dog owners have to deal with is their dogs jumping on people. Sometimes the owner of a jumping maniac may stop having visitors because the jumping is so intense. Jumping is natural for certain breeds, but your dog must be able to behave acceptably, both in your home and in public.

Why Do Dogs Jump?

Jumping up on people is one way to get attention, and since dogs do what works, the problem can perpetuate itself to the point where the dog jumps constantly. It is important to understand where jumping comes from and what causes dogs to do this. Dogs in a pack situation greet each other face to face, and after a few licks and sniffs they have decided whether they are friend or foe, and they proceed from there to fight or play. When they have been away from their group for a prolonged period of time, they greet each other with a combination of licking and sniffing to re-establish their status within the group and find out where their family members have been.

What about people who invite my dog to jump?
Being consistent is a very important part of training. Be clear about what the rules are, and be a strong advocate for your dog. It is imperative that while you are teaching your dog alternate behaviour, no one, however well-intentioned, sabotages that plan.

When pet dogs jump on us, they are trying to get to our faces in order to greet us in a similar manner. This natural behaviour, which is actually a gesture of affection and happiness, can easily scare or offend strangers – or owners – with the result that the dog becomes isolated from the very people he is trying so hard to be with. Dogs that are exuberant greeters need to be taught appropriate manners around visitors so that they can be part of family life. After all, jumping works: it gets people to pay attention to them!

The Welcoming Committee

Many people don't like it when their dog jumps on them, and place a lot of emphasis on how to stop the action of jumping. In truth they are barking up the wrong tree. It is far more effective to define what you prefer the dog to do instead. It is more likely that you will reach your target if you know what behaviour you are looking for so that you can reward your dog for performing the right action.

Emphasizing what you want the dog to do by noticing it and rewarding it will help you achieve your goal of a better-mannered pet. Most people choose to have their dogs Sit and Stay when they say hello to people; this is a clear goal for the dog to accomplish, and can be used in place of jumping. You should teach your dog how to Sit and Stay, and reward it generously when he does it around people.

Build a History

Rewarding your dog for the right behaviour over and over again makes the correct action a more likely choice when your dog is faced with greeting new people. Dogs do what works; if sitting is rewarded when he greets new people, he will try sitting as his first choice. This is where knowing what you want your dog to do comes in handy. If a Sit/Stay is what you want the dog to do instead of jumping on guests, then you must reward it often and handsomely.

The way to change unwanted behaviour is to heavily reinforce the appropriate action and keep your dog from practising the wrong behaviour as much as possible. For instance, when someone is visiting, keep a lead on your dog so that you can step on it whenever necessary to prevent your dog from jumping. Click and treat the dog any time he sits without being asked to. Ask the visitor to go away and try again, but this time, ask for Sit only once. If it happens, click and treat; if it doesn't, the visitor goes away. The dog thus learns by trial and error that if he wants the visitor to stay, he must sit, and if he doesn't sit, the guest will leave.

If your dog has only a vague idea of what the commands Sit and Stay mean, it is essential that you go over them with him somewhere where it is quiet and there are few distractions. You can't expect a dog that can barely Sit and Stay where there are no distractions to Sit and Stay when there are people to jump on.

This exercise assumes that you have taught your dog to respond to the Sit command and you have practised it in different environments with lots of different types of distractions. Apply the Ten in a Row rule to see if your dog really knows how to Sit in each new environment. Do this by asking your dog to Sit ten times in a row without a click or treat (you can praise each correct repetition). If he doesn't get ten out of ten correct, you have more training to do. Go back to drilling and practising with him with this distraction until he can pass the test.

Two Golden
Retrievers and
a German
Shepherd

Provide Lots of Opportunities to Practise

There is nothing like repetition for aiding the learning process. The more opportunities the learner has to practise the desirable behaviour and get rewarded for it, the more likely he is to perform this new action in real life. Having short, interesting training sessions – with lots of changes in training and delicious treats, toys and games as rewards – will set you on your way to having a dog that knows what to do and does it because you have taught him. Setting up lots of training sessions where you practise different types of greetings will help your dog gain the experience he needs to have good manners anywhere.

Lots of different things are happening when a dog is learning how to greet people without putting his paws on them. Changing these actions slowly enough to maintain the dog's response to the command, yet with enough variation to challenge him a bit, is the key to successful training. Every session will take you that much closer to your target of a well-mannered pet. Some of the training scenarios for teaching or practising a polite greeting are:

· A person greeting you and your dog while you are out on a walk.
· A visitor at the front door.
· A person greeting your dog at the pet shop, the vet or the groomer.
· A person with a dog greeting you and your dog.
· A person sitting somewhere and you and your dog approaching them.
· A person walking up to you while you are sitting with your dog.
· A child greeting your dog.
· A person with food greeting your dog.

The more combinations of circumstances that you train for, the more reliable your dog will be and the more likely he will be to perform Sit/Stay instead of jumping. The key to getting things to run smoothly is to not change more than one part at a time. Don't be afraid to go back and review Sit/Stay in places where your dog has never been or places where he has a history of jumping and bad behaviour. Start off in places where you can get your dog's attention easily, and gradually build up to places that are very distracting for him.

When trying to get rid of undesirable behaviour, you must consistently set your dog up to succeed. Limit his options, give him every chance to get it right, and reward him when he does. Setting your dog up to succeed will help your dog learn what is expected of him and make him a more pleasant companion to have around.

Define Your Dog's Greatest Distraction

Working out what makes your dog lose control in different environments will help you break your training sessions down into smaller parts, making it easier for your dog to be successful. It is important that you do *not* try to train your dog when he is totally out of control, because he isn't thinking about learning or paying attention. It is a more valuable use of your time to take it slowly and add in one distraction at a time until your dog learns to ignore all distractions and stay focused on you instead.

Take a minute to think about where you are likely to meet people when you are out on your walk, and try to determine the circumstances around his jumping. Does your dog go crazy when he meets new people while you are out for a walk? Are they passing you on the street or approaching you while you are sitting somewhere? What scenario distracts him the most, and what are the circumstances leading up to it? Some of the distractions that dogs find irresistible are: visitors at the front door, children coming home from school, relatives visiting and people with dogs at the park. Defining the circumstances around which your dog loses control is useful, as it gives you an idea of where to start and what you will be working towards.

Just as your dog did not start jumping overnight, he will not just suddenly stop. Taking the time to recruit your family and friends to be mock visitors will allow you to set up training sessions that mimic real life, and will help your dog learn that he must Sit and Stay in front of people instead of jumping on them.

If your dog is totally out of control around people who come to the door, for instance, you could break down the distraction for your dog into smaller parts. One of your training sessions could start by practising Sit and Stay in front of the closed door with no visitor; then you could add a family member as the visitor; then put the family member outside the door; then add a knock or the doorbell; and eventually build up to being able to practise this with real guests. Breaking the hardest distractions down into small training sessions that introduce one aspect of the distraction at a time is the key to helping your dog learn a new response in a stimulating environment.

If your dog is more of an outdoor kind of jumper that gets overexcited in play and starts trying to mug you for the ball, using a lead might help you manage this behaviour while you reward him for doing something more appropriate instead. When the dog is excited, ask for Sit once. If he sits, click and throw the ball; if not, tell him 'too bad' and walk away for a minute or two, then try again after a couple of minutes. The click marks the action of sitting on the first try, and the dog's reward is the toss of the ball to him.

What better way is there to teach your dog some self-control than to make the throwing of the ball dependent upon his response to the Sit command? Once he catches on, even a really energetic dog will love this game. Using games is a great way to enrich your relationship with your dog while fine-tuning his response to basic obedience commands and general control issues.

Avoid Punishing Jumping

Punishment is tempting and seems to work at first, because the bad behaviour of jumping goes away. But really, all punishment does is stop the behaviour temporarily; it does not instruct the dog to choose the right actions, nor does it replace jumping with anything but the prediction of being punished. Putting this kind of emphasis on punishment for jumping can backfire with sensitive dogs, making them afraid to greet people and suspicious of hands or knees. Dogs that have aggressive tendencies may actually turn and bite the person who is correcting them, causing a much more serious problem than the one you started with. Remember that punishment comes too late to teach the dog anything, and if poorly timed, it may teach your dog that visitors mean he's about to get punished.

Instead, set your dog up to do the right thing: Sit instead of jump. Make sure you notice him when he's not jumping, and reward him with lots of attention! A wise trainer once said, 'You get what you pay attention to'. Start paying attention to what's going well, and more good things will start happening than you ever imagined.

Some dogs actually view yelling, scolding, or pushing as a reward — because, after all, it *is* attention. Any attention for the wrong behaviour will perpetuate that behaviour and make it stronger.

Remember to Manage the Behaviour

Part of every training programme to cure behaviour problems includes management. Here, this isn't training as much as it is prevention. You are preventing the dog from practising an action that drives you mad. Part of managing jumping might involve keeping your dog in another room when visitors arrive until you are ready and able to train him.

Even if you only do minimal management, you should be putting your foot on the dog's lead to prevent him from jumping any time there are people around. Each time you fail to do this and your dog jumps on someone, you are putting money in the bank for this action, and it will become stronger with time. Keep a lead by your front door for ready access whenever visitors arrive. Keep your foot on your dog's lead whenever you go into the pet shop or veterinary surgery or stop to talk to someone on the street. The fewer opportunities your dog has to jump on people, the more swiftly he will learn to sit instead.

Teaching Sit/Stay With Duration

The duration of an action refers to how long the dog has to do the action in order to get rewarded. To avoid jumping, you want the dog to Sit and Stay for an extended period of time. You'll want to extend this period of time slowly until your dog will hold the position without trying to jump for one to two minutes. Eventually you'll also want to get your dog to perform Sit/Stay despite the distractions of people or other dogs.

Although you learned how to shape behaviour for Sit/Stay in Chapter 5, take a moment to review it in these circumstances:

1. Use a treat to lure his nose up, and move your hand slightly back.
2. When his bottom hits the floor, click and treat.
3. Repeat this until your dog is performing Sit regularly when he sees your hand above his head.
4. Practise without the treat in your hand. Click when his bottom hits the floor, and follow up with a treat.
5. Put the treats down and repeat, running with the dog to get the treat after you click for him to sit down.
6. Introduce distractions or train somewhere new, and go back to the beginning if necessary.
7. Change the distractions to mimic the ones that happen in real life: people meeting at the park, on the street or at the pet shop, as well as at home.
8. Build duration in a non-distracting environment and increase it to double the amount of time you'll think you need. To build duration, simply count extra seconds between clicks and treats until your dog is easily waiting for 20–40 seconds for his click and treat.

Building in a long duration for Sit/Stay will help you in public when there are lots of distractions. In practice, you may be working on 30 seconds, and in real life your dog may give you only 15 seconds, but it's a start. Even 15 seconds will give you time to react quickly enough to keep your dog from putting his paws on a visitor.

Creating a Sitting Maniac

It isn't hard to get a dog hooked on an action that works, but it does take time and thought along the way. One great activity to keep things interesting for puppies is the Sit for a Treat game. To play this game in a group-dog setting, take your puppy off his lead and wander around the room greeting other puppies. Approach one of the other puppies with your dog and get the owner of that puppy to ask her dog to Sit, asking only once. If the puppy sits on the first try, click and treat and move on to the next dog. If the puppy doesn't sit on the first try, simply walk away and ignore the puppy, moving on to the next one. Sometimes if the puppies are very high-energy it takes a while for them to catch on, but soon several puppies will be sitting perfectly in the middle of the room while the rest are running all over the place around them. One or two lone puppies may be sitting stoically, refusing to move for anything – they know exactly what they need to do to get people to pay attention to them.

Boston Terrier
lounges on
his bed

Play this game at home by inviting friends or relatives over and doing the same exercise. Ask everyone to wander around, armed with clickers and treats, and take turns giving only one command to Sit and clicking and treating your dog for responding on the first try. In a short time, you will see your dog going from person to person, sitting as fast as his rear end will let him to earn his goodie. Use your dog's dinner for this exercise if you like; it's a great way for him to practise his good manners and earn his dinner doing it.

Jumping is a natural behaviour gone askew through inappropriate rewarding of the wrong behaviour. There is nothing difficult about teaching your dog to Sit instead of jump; it just needs to be practised in increasingly distracting environments until your dog adopts it as second nature. Remember, as with any bad habit or addiction (yes, some dogs are so good at jumping that they have become addicted to it), it takes time and patience to change unwanted behaviour. Through lots of repetitions and opportunities to practise the right training you will find that your dog will be sitting for attention instead of jumping at people. Owning a dog that knows how to greet guests politely makes it easier to take your dog anywhere and have him actively involved in your life.

The absence of acknowledgment for undesirable behaviour can be a powerful message. Dogs expect the people they jump on to acknowledge them in some way. Train the people in your family to turn and walk away from your jumping dog without any contact.

CHAPTER 18
Dogs That Dig

oes your back garden look like an archaeological dig? Some dogs dig huge craters that resemble a dirt swimming pool, while other canine archaeologists prefer to leave dozens of smaller holes, perfectly conducive to breaking an ankle. Regardless of your dog's digging style, most dogs find digging a pleasurable and self-rewarding activity, and once they get going it can be hard to stop them.

Why Do Dogs Dig?

Most of the terrier breeds were bred to dig out vermin, mice, rats and moles, and so for some dogs digging is instinctive. Generally, however, dogs dig for a variety of reasons, ranging from boredom, frustration and lack of exercise to a real need to stay cool on a hot day. Looking at some of the reasons for digging may help you get to the bottom of your dog's digging problem.

Boredom

A bored dog is a ticket to destruction. A dog with nothing to do will bark, howl, chew, destroy and dig. Digging is a great stress-reliever, and digging up whatever treasures he can find is well worth the effort. If you think that boredom may be your dog's motive for digging, take steps to improve his environment now. Provide lots of safe, interesting toys, and rotate them regularly. Take him for a romp in the woods, let him play with other dogs at the park, or teach him tricks. Anything you add will help to alleviate some of the boredom that is causing him to dig. A great way to lose boredom, in addition to physical exercise, is mental exercise. Some ideas for mental workouts are:

- Stuff Kong toys with dog food and peanut butter, and let your dog work out how to get the food out.
- Freeze the toy to make this an even cooler challenge on a hot day.
- Invite a friend's dog to spend the afternoon playing and wrestling with your dog.
- Buy interesting toys for your dog, and rotate them weekly so that your dog always has something new to play with.
- Put treats in different places in the garden for your dog to find.
- Put your dog's meals in a treat-dispensing toy and let him work for his dinner.
- Put peanut butter or cream cheese on the inside of the shaft of a marrow bone (uncooked) and let your dog have fun licking it out.
- Make some agility equipment – tunnels, ramps, jumps, etc. – and teach your dog to negotiate them with and without your help.

Remember that dogs need a variety of play, training and exercise to be happy, healthy and contented family pets. When behaviour is extreme, such as digging or barking, it usually is an advertisement for needing more of something. In most cases, it's that the dog is bored and frustrated because he does not get enough exercise or quality time with his owner.

Frustration

If your dog is unsupervised in a fenced area or dog pen, he may start to dig out of frustration. Your dog can see and hear people passing by, but can't get to where the action is. A dog that is frustrated by being confined for too long will often try to dig his way to freedom. Don't leave your dog unattended for long periods of time, and stimulate his environment by hiding toys packed with his dinner and peanut butter, or hiding bones and things to chew in the area where he is confined. Go out and play with him, and distract him from digging if he does it while you are present.

Playtime with other dogs is a great stress-easer and an essential part of the day for the average active dog. Invite a dog friend over on a regular basis to help you tire out your active dog, or consider enrolling your pooch in well-run day kennels.

If your dog tries to dig out of the garden, you may want to bury 6mm (1/4in) mesh wire along the fence line to make it impossible to dig past a certain depth. Most dogs become discouraged once they hit something that won't let them dig any deeper, and find other pursuits. The best way to alleviate frustration is to spend more time with your dog and provide him with more things to think about.

Exercise

If there is one thing that can save you time in the long run, it's providing your dog with enough exercise. The more opportunities your dog gets to run, chase, swim, wrestle, roll and romp, the less energy he has to dig holes. If you own an active dog – and most diggers are very active – he will need at least one to three hours of exercise daily. Whether you take him for long runs in the woods, allow him time off the lead to play with other dogs or enroll him in day care kennels, he needs his exercise. Make sure you're doing everything you can to meet his basic needs before you complain about the digging.

Provide Shade

Not paying attention to a dog's basic need to be cool on a hot day may contribute to your dog's digging problem. On a hot day, a dog's instincts tell him to find a cool, dry place to rest. In the absence of adequate shade, a dog will often dig a hole and lie in it. Digging a hole to lie in is a natural way for the dog to cool himself on a hot day. If your dog is outdoors in hot weather, provide plenty of shade, shelter and water, or consider leaving him indoors with air conditioning on or a fan running. Each dog has a different sensitivity to heat and cold; observe your dog for signs that it's too hot or too cold for him outdoors. Here are some ideas for keeping cool on a hot day:

- Give your dog a frozen Kong stuffed with peanut butter and his dog food.
- Set up a beach umbrella and a paddling pool in the garden.
- Put some ice cubes in his water bowl.
- Freeze some dog biscuits in water and put them in the paddling pool.
- Get a special sun-reflecting cover and secure it over your dog's outdoor pen.

For the sake of his comfort – and health – you need to provide your dog with plenty of water and shade on hot days. Make sure that even an active dog is not allowed to overdo it with play and exercise. Try taking your dog out for exercise early in the morning or after the sun goes down, to prevent heatstroke.

Legal Digging Zone

Dogs whose genetics tell them to dig need alternative outlets for their enthusiastic escapades. Replacing the inappropriate behaviour with a more appropriate action is the only permanent solution. If digging comes naturally to these dogs, why not provide a safe, legal place for them to dig by making a digging pit? A digging pit can be any size, but 1.2 x 1.2m (4 x 4ft) for small dogs and 2.4 x 2.4m (8 x 8ft) for larger breeds can be a general guideline. Use garden timbers to make a box shape, and fill the box with sand. You may actually want to dig out the existing soil and make a bed of stone for the bottom to supply good drainage. This way, regardless of the climate, it won't become a mud puddle in inclement weather. Fill the rest of the pit with play sand, the kind used in children's sandpits. Use a metal rake to evenly distribute the sand.

You may want to invest in a metal rake so that you can clear any uncovered treasure from the digging pit and keep the sand loose and inviting. You may also want to add fresh sand regularly to provide plenty of places to hide new goodies.

Now comes the fun part! Bury toys, bones, dried meat, dog biscuits, balls and other surprises for your dog to find. Make some of the treasures easy to find, others more difficult. The more of a digger your dog is, the more challenging you should make the treasure hunt. Once a week you should hide new treasures and rake the pit to remove any old biscuits, bones or other used treats. Think creatively about what you choose and bury, and your active dog will know exactly where to dig to find the good things. Here are some ideas for buried treasure:

· Hard dog biscuits
· Kongs stuffed with peanut butter and treats
· Marrow bones (real ones from the butcher, uncooked, are safest)
· Dried meat sticks, bones and chips
· Pigs' ears (available form pet shops and markets) smeared with cream cheese inside a paper bag
· A small cardboard jewellery box filled with treats
· A cardboard ice-cream box with treats or a chew toy inside
· A favourite toy, such as a ball or a stuffed toy, hidden in a paper bag and then buried

Regardless of the treasure, make sure it is something that your dog can safely have unattended. Experiment while you are watching him to be sure he doesn't eat anything that he shouldn't (such as the paper bag you've hidden the tennis ball in). A certain amount of shredding is fine; you just don't want him eating the entire empty ice-cream container.

What about filling in existing holes?
There are many theories about what to do about the holes that your dog has already dug. Some people leave the holes alone, and the dog then only digs in the holes he's made. Other people put large rocks in the existing holes before filling them in. Experiment to see what works best for your particular dog.

Two solutions for digging that work for some people are to bury some of the dog's faeces in each hole, or bury 6mm (¹/₄in) mesh wire about 25–50mm (1–2in) under the soil. In the first case, the dog uncovers something he thinks he's buried before. In the latter, when he hits the mesh, he can't go any deeper and gives up.

Regardless of what you try as a solution to stop your canine archaeologist from turning your garden into something off Time Team, the only way to really stop a digger is not to give him the opportunity to dig in inappropriate places. Supervise him closely, don't leave him unattended in the garden, and consider building him a digging area of his own. A dog that enjoys digging will love the chance to practise it legally.

You'll have noted that there are no suggestions here regarding punishment. Excessive digging is a symptom of a larger problem. Digging is the dog's way of releasing pent-up energy, boredom and frustration. Alleviate your dog's boredom by signing him up for fun obedience classes or by taking a class to teach him tricks or agility, and be sure to regularly provide stimulating toys that he doesn't see every day. Be creative in providing lots of stimulating activities for your dog, and you will be rewarded with a calm, more contented family pet – and a lot fewer holes in your back garden.

CHAPTER 19

Lunging and On-Lead Aggression

Dog aggression sometimes gets its start from inappropriate lead training in a young dog. Adult dogs find it rude when an adolescent dog jumps on them or gets into their space uninvited. The human end of the lead often makes the problem worse by making the lead too short and not paying attention to what the dog is doing.

Leads Can Cause Aggressive Behaviour

When dogs are off the lead and encounter other dogs or stimuli, they are free to get away, display a 'don't bother me' attitude or simply invite the other dog to play. Dogs on leads cannot show these same emotions, and feel more cornered and threatened. Leads and the owners who hold them can make it impossible for dogs to give the appropriate signals to each other, and tend to get in the way of communicating, rather than helping the dogs get along. Dog owners who fear their dog's reaction to other dogs often don't help matters because they tense up and tighten the lead, signalling to the dog that trouble lies ahead.

Owner Manners

People with dogs on leads tend to approach each other head-on, whereas dogs normally approach one another in a curved half-circle. Approaching head-to-head is a combative signal that says you mean business and may want to fight. Your dog may recognize another dog's rank and lower himself ever so slightly to signal to the other dog that he means no harm. As a human, however, you pull yourself and the lead upright when you see the other dog coming. Pulling up on the lead changes your dog's body posture into a more threatening stance, causing the other dog to react and your dog to become defensive. The higher-ranking dog is taken by surprise and attacks your dog for changing his mind and giving the wrong message at the last moment. No wonder it is difficult for dogs on leads to get along!

What should I do when my dog greets another dog on the lead?
It is crucial to keep a loose lead when allowing your dog to greet another dog who is on the lead. Always ask first to make sure the other dog is usually friendly, and let the dogs approach each other from the side, rather than the front.

The person holding the lead is often the one responsible for the greeting going badly, as he or she inadvertently pulls the dog into a more dominant posture, which sends exactly the wrong message to the other dog. The source of the problem comes down to poor lead training on the dog's part and not enough control on the owner's part.

Dog Manners

Dogs that, in play, launch themselves at other dogs on the lead are also sending the wrong message. Jumping on other dogs that are trapped on a lead and can't get away is rude and bad dog manners. Dogs that do this are often corrected sharply by other dogs, and their owners often mistake this for true aggression. If this scenario is repeated enough, the friendly dog starts to learn to be defensive and the beginnings of lead aggression result. The reality here is that the jumping dog has had poor lead training and has broken the cardinal rule: no jumping on an adult dog.

Lead training for well-socialized dogs includes not pulling or lunging around other dogs, sitting when greeting another dog and owner, and only going to other dogs with permission.

No dog on a lead should have to put up with another dog jumping on him, even in play. It is important for you, as the owner of your dog, to make sure that you have appropriate control of your dog around other dogs. The more well-trained your dog is, the better accepted he will be by other dogs on lead, and people as well. Too many bad experiences will make the dog wary of approaching other dogs on the lead and cause reflexive, defensive aggression.

The Lead

The best type of lead for walking an aggressive dog is a 2m (6ft) nylon or leather lead. A dog with lunging and aggression problems should not be on an extendable lead, nor should he ever be off the lead around other dogs. A 2m (6ft) lead allows you to control your dog and keep him close to you. The way you hold the lead is important to your dog's progress as well. In general, it is best to hold it with two hands, one hand through the loop end and the other about halfway down the length, keeping the dof on your left side. This allows your dog a little slack but not so much that he can lunge ahead of you without you being able to easily prevent it. Holding the lead too tightly so that your dog has barely enough room to move is not recommended. Don't force your dog to walk right next to you; let him have a little slack. The slacker the lead is (without letting him get too far ahead of you), the less confined and cornered he will feel when he sees another dog.

When the lead is attached to a Halti head halter, remember that it is self-correcting and does not require you to jerk or pull. If your dog tries to lunge, the action will naturally pull his head to the ground. Before your dog lunges, you should try to get his attention back on you and move in the opposite direction. Make sure you are prepared not only to move away from the other dog, but to click and treat your dog for moving with you. Throwing the reward on the ground is also a good idea, because it may be a little more interesting for your dog, giving you the time you need to get him under control while the other dog goes on its way.

The way you hold the lead is an important part of successful interaction. The looser the lead, the more able your dog is to show other dogs that he means no harm. Maintaining slack in the lead will enable your dog to discriminate friendly dogs from not-so-friendly ones. Many problems start with a lead that is too tight and a dog with no lead training.

Lead Manners

For dogs with good social skills that get into trouble while on a lead, it is worth taking simple steps to help improve on-lead training. First of all, you need to use the right equipment. There are lots of products on the market today that help you to control your dog's pulling. The problem with these devices is that they fool you into thinking your dog suddenly knows not to pull on his lead, then, as soon as the device is removed, the dog goes back to pulling. The important thing to keep in mind is that all training collars and devices are just that, devices. They facilitate training; they do not replace it. Regardless of what piece of training equipment you use, you must click and treat your dog for not pulling and eventually name it and wean the dog off the treats, clicker and collar.

Golden
Retriever
saying he's
'sorry'

The mistake most people make is that they put training collars on dogs and then expect the dogs to somehow magically work out what they want them to do. If you don't reward your dog for the right behaviour, you will not get the right behaviour. When using a training collar, you must reward the dog for walking with you, or the dog will have no idea what is expected of him. The way the training collar works is that when the dog pulls, the handler jerks and releases the lead to make pulling an unpleasant choice. The dog is supposed to stop pulling (at least for a second). The dog must then be rewarded when it stops pulling, or no real learning will occur.

Most dogs that are not rewarded for the appropriate action end up thinking the exercise is 'Run to the end of the lead, your owner gives you a yank, go back to her side, and run to the end of the lead again.' Not all dogs will respond this way, however. Some very sensitive dogs will fall apart the first time they are corrected and never try to pull again, but they are doing so out of fear, not because they have learned that you want them next to you. Sensitive dogs should probably not wear a training collar in the first place, since they learn quickly through much more gentle methods.

The head halter (see Chapter 15) works very well while training your dog not to pull. The lead clip is under the dog's chin, so there is no constriction of the windpipe when the dog pulls. These collars are also self-correcting. When the dog pulls forwards, the head is forced down, effectively stopping the dog from moving forwards. This means that there is no need to jerk on the lead or correct your dog; in fact, doing so may damage his neck. The head halter teaches a dog not to pull by operating on several principles:

1. A dog that pulls while wearing a head halter ends up with his nose to the ground and can not walk forwards until he puts slack in the lead.
2. Since the halter fits over the dog's neck and muzzle, it gives the handler complete control over the dog's head.
3. If you control where the head goes, the body must follow.
4. The way the collar fits (over the back of the neck and over the top of the muzzle) mimics what a mother dog does when she disciplines her puppies.
5. Because the owner now has complete control, many dogs learn to trust their handlers and pay more attention to them.

The head halter is a must for teaching on-lead manners. When used correctly, this device will not only prevent lunging, but also lower the dog's head and body carriage, which will make him less likely to provoke other dogs. The simple fact that you now control the dog's head is enough to prevent future repetitions of the problem.

Reward the Right Behaviour

Teach your dog to be polite on a lead around other dogs by clicking and treating him for approaching dogs sideways instead of head-on, for turning his head away instead of staring, and for offering a play Bow instead of jumping on the other dog. The play Bow (see Chapter 6), a natural action in which the dog puts its chest and belly close to the ground and the rear in the air, is a command you can use on cue so that you can ask your dog to Bow when greeting another dog.

A dog that isn't getting enough exercise is sure to be badly behaved when on a lead. His built-up energy has to come out somehow and will manifest itself in lunging, leaping and frantic on-lead behaviour. If this describes your dog, provide more exercise and outlets for his pent-up energy and exuberance for life.

Remember that when teaching a dog to heel when on a lead, the most important point is to not allow your dog to pull. When your dog pulls and you follow, you are reinforcing your dog for pulling to get where he wants to go. If your dog is a few years old, he probably already has a substantial history of pulling and lunging, and you will have some training to do if you are going to compete with that.

The first step is to make lots of turns so that you are always in the lead and your dog has to closely watch you to see where you are going to end up next. Changing direction and clicking and treating your dog for catching up is the key to teaching him that being next to you is better than pulling or lagging behind. With lots of repetition and changes in direction and distractions, your dog will start to understand that walking on a lead means walking next to you, not pulling you down the street.

Teach Your Dog to Leave It

Leave It means that the dog stops and looks back at his handler. This definition will help you in many situations, from your dog chasing a cat or squirrel across a busy street to lunging at another dog or person. Leave It means 'Stop what you are doing or thinking about doing, and look in my direction'. Once your dog is looking at you, you have a much greater chance of getting him to respond to your directions to Heel, Come, Lie Down or whatever. Teaching your dog to Leave It is probably the most important thing your dog must learn if he is going to be safe to walk in public places. The faster and more reliable the response to this command, the better your control will be.

For dogs that lack social skills, training your dog to Leave It will be your best management tool. The longer the duration of looking at you that your dog can master, the more able you will be to control him around other dogs and people. Leave It is an invaluable command for dogs that lunge at other dogs on leads. When teaching Leave It, it is important to catch the dog before he starts to lunge and bark.

Once the dog is barking and lunging, he is no longer in learning mode, and no amount of yelling or correction will get him there. You must beat him to this highly charged emotional state by interrupting him before he really notices the other dog and then reversing direction so that he moves with you. Click and treat your dog for moving away from the other dog and going with you. One way to increase your dog's enthusiasm for turning away is to throw a handful of treats in the grass so that he has to hunt them up. The time it takes for him to do this will give the other dog and owner enough time to go by you. When he's finished, you can continue on your walk.

Because following you and leaving the distraction is a new pattern of behaviour, you'll have to practise it over and over again until your dog does it almost automatically. If your timing is off and you don't turn him around or distract him in time, he will explode into a frenzy of barking. There is nothing you can do at this point except to just get through it and try again the next time. By not shouting at or correcting the dog you will at least not be making an issue of the undesirable behaviour.

Here are the steps to teaching your dog to leave another dog:

1. Use familiar dogs at first so that you can completely control your training session and the dogs. Get your helper and 'distraction dog' to start on the opposite side of the street.
2. Make sure you interrupt your dog when he's thinking about lunging or barking. Interrupt him by saying his name and then turning 180 degrees in the opposite direction. Click and treat him for turning with you.
3. If your dog doesn't turn with you, it means that you are too close to the distraction dog; move away from the other dog by a metre or so and try again.
4. Throw a handful of goodies for him to eat after you click so that you make it well worth his while to pay attention to you.
5. Once your dog is ignoring the other dog and turning with you easily, shorten the distance by getting the dog to approach on the same side of the street and repeat from the start.
6. Build up to being able to let the distraction dog pass within a few metres with no reaction from your dog.
7. Change the distractions by using different dogs and changing where you practise until your dog can ignore any dog anywhere.

For training purposes, the 'distraction dog' should be a completely reliable, well-socialized adult dog that will not react to the aggressive dog in any way. It will also help to get the distraction dog to wear a head halter to help the aggressive dog perceive him as non-threatening. Repeat the training until your dog is looking to you when he sees other dogs.

Set Reasonable Targets

Dogs with few or no social skills are never going to be totally friendly or trustworthy with other dogs. There is no such thing as resocializing an adult dog that has no experience with other dogs. Doing so would be dangerous and most likely end in injury to dogs or the humans that interfered. The best that can be done with dogs like this is to set a reasonable target. Your aim might be to have your dog like other dogs, but a more reasonable one might be to get him to respond immediately to your command to Leave It.

Teaching your dog appropriate lead manners of not lunging or barking and turning his head away from other dogs, rather than staring them down, will mean you can take him more places and be able to control him. Acknowledge that although you would like your dog to get along with other dogs, your dog is perfectly content to not have any contact with them. Don't force your own desire for your dog to socialize; he may feel he has as many friends as he needs, and no amount of pushing on your part will change that. Respect what your dog is trying to tell you, and keep him safe around other dogs.

If you have a young puppy, let him meet and play with as many different kinds of puppies and adult dogs as you can. The window for getting a dog to socialize with other dogs is short, between the ages of eight and 18 weeks. As the window closes, your dog is less open to new experiences and less likely to be social with other dogs.

Make the Commitment

The worst thing you can do with this type of problem is to be in a rush. Your dog did not get this way overnight, and no one thing you do is going to magically change your dog's opinion of other dogs. This process of teaching appropriate manners to a dog with no social experience around dogs is time-consuming. You must be totally committed to helping improve your dog's behaviour in order to even start to cure the problem. A half-hearted attempt to change your dog's behaviour will not help you reach your target.

In order to make progress, you will have to do hundreds of repetitions of Leave It and put lots of time into practising keeping the lead loose. This is a long-term programme; don't expect miracles overnight. As with anything in life, you get out of it what you put into it. If you practise diligently and set reasonable goals, you will eventually be rewarded by a more enjoyable walking companion.

Lack of Socialization

So far, you've read about dogs with fairly good social skills but with bad lead training. What about dogs that have not been socialized with other dogs? Dogs that lack social experience are a more serious problem than dogs with bad lead training. The reason for this is simple: dogs with social skills know that not all dogs are going to attack them and have had good experiences with other dogs. Dogs that have not been socialized with other dogs have nothing to go on, and every dog they see, friendly or not, is perceived as a threat. Dogs that have no canine social skills are not, and never will be, socially normal.

Socializing a dog with other dogs must happen when the dog is a puppy of between eight and 18 weeks of age. If the puppy is not around other puppies and adult dogs at this age, it will never be socially normal with other dogs. Socialization is like training, however, and must be fostered and maintained throughout the animal's entire life; if dogs don't get to practise their social skills, they lose them. Dogs need to play with others of their own kind to learn the ins and outs of acceptable behaviour and appropriate body language. Without these experiences, they begin to act suspiciously and aggressively towards other dogs. Most people notice that this problem is even worse when their dog is on a lead, because the dog feels trapped and can't escape.

The Door Is Open Technique

Classical conditioning can be a very powerful tool in getting faster and more reliable results in your training programme. The Open and Closed Door technique uses the principles of classical conditioning to change the way your dog feels about other dogs who are restrained. Classical conditioning deals with associations (see Chapter 13). The presence of other dogs means that the door is open and all kinds of good things happen, including affection, attention and treats, regardless of the dog's behaviour. (He can be lunging or barking hysterically, and you continue to drop treats like it is Christmas). When the other dog disappears, so do the treats and games and attention; in fact, the handler gives the dog the cold shoulder.

> When using classical conditioning to change your dog's behaviour, you'll want to be sure you keep your distance so that the other dogs can't come right up to you. Be sure your dog is on the lead and at enough of a distance so as to give him every opportunity for success.

Classical conditioning tries to change the way the dog feels about having other dogs around by associating other dogs with good things. The drawback of this technique is that it takes the animal time to realize the association between the good things and the offending presence of another dog. The way to use this technique effectively is to practise frequently so as to give your dog an increasingly big savings account for liking the sight of other dogs. Eventually your dog will like having other dogs around because it means that he is going to have access to all the things he loves.

Here's how it works in real life:

- Choose a spot where other dogs are likely to pass by, and bring all of your very best rewards. This can range from cheese, liver and diced sausage to tennis balls, tug toys and squeaky toys.
- When other dogs are within sight, regardless of your dog's behaviour, the door is open. You bounce the ball, throw it, roll it and shower your dog with treats, toys and attention. As soon as the dog is out of sight, the door is closed. You put the goodies away, step on the lead and ignore your dog completely for at least a full two minutes.
- When another dog comes by, you again open the door; when it disappears, the door is closed.

· After this is repeated over and over again, your dog is going to learn a new reaction to other dogs. He is going to learn that when other dogs are present good things happen, and when they go the fun is over.

Lunging and aggression when on a lead is a fairly serious behaviour problem, one that requires lots of consistent practice in order to change it. It is not something that will go away with just a little training, and the training needs to be constantly kept up to scratch. Dogs revert back to old habits if you don't consistently reward the right training. Consider this behaviour problem as one that needs constant maintenance to ensure that the dog adopts the new action of turning away as a habit.

Remember that bad habits are hard to get rid of because they are comfortable (think of eating the wrong foods, or smoking). If new behaviour is going to replace old actions, there must be some planning involved and time set aside for practice. Keep in mind that, as with any old habit, there will be regression and mistakes. Plan for them so that you're ready to get back on track and so that they don't totally put you off. With time, patience, love and training, you can make any dog a better companion.

CHAPTER 20

Canine
Social Skills

ogs are social animals that learn to
interact and get along with each
other by playing together from a
very young age. The best way for them to
learn how to get along is for them to play
with lots of other dogs during the most
impressionable time in their lives, the first
eight to 18 weeks of age.

Socialization Versus Training

Training a dog the basics of Sit, Stay and Come can be accomplished at any age, but the ideal time to socialize your dog with other dogs, people and new experiences is between the ages of eight and 18 weeks. Once a puppy is 18 weeks old, he is less open to new experiences and begins to gravitate towards the familiar rather than explore the new. You must, of course, continue to give your dog social experiences beyond the age of 18 weeks, but if you don't start before then you are sentencing your dog to a life of nervous and suspicious reactions to other dogs, new experiences and people.

Socializing a dog is an investment of time and energy and should include not only experiences with other dogs but with people of all shapes and sizes, and new experiences as well. It isn't good enough to just show up in public; careful planning is required to make sure your dog has positive experiences that will benefit him for a lifetime. Giving your dog a varied experience of life will teach him from an early age to cope with sounds, sights, smells, new people and a variety of breeds and mixed breeds of dogs. By making an effort to socialize your dog, you are increasing his ability to learn how to behave around people and other dogs, and you are giving him the best chance of becoming an adult dog that is well-mannered and friendly. A good solid social experience will benefit him for a lifetime.

Although it's imperative to begin socialization around the first month of a puppy's life, it's also important to keep at it to introduce him to new experiences. Before socialization can really begin, take your puppy to a vet at about eight weeks for a health check and vaccination regime.

Dogs have a critical socialization window during which time they should meet at least 100 people and 100 other dogs and puppies. The window opens some time around the second week of life, when the puppies first open their eyes, and the window starts to close around the 18th week. This doesn't mean that socialization stops there. It must continue beyond this point, but it means that your puppy is most impressionable at this age and can accept new experiences more easily than an older dog. The more positive experiences with people and other dogs that your puppy has during this time, the more willing he will be to accept and get along with people and dogs for the rest of his life. You can make or break a dog's potential by offering the right socialization at the right time.

Socialization is not the same for every dog. There are as many personality types among dogs as there are among people: some are outgoing, some are shy, some are overbearing, some are vocal, some are physical, and so on. A puppy's playing style will often determine what types of puppies he should play with in order to learn the right ways to socialize and get along with other dogs.

Socializing Your Dog With Other Dogs

Socialization to other dogs is perhaps the most overlooked aspect of a dog's experience. The more dogs and puppies a young dog meets, the better able he will be to get along with any dog, anywhere. Not supplying your dog with the skills with which to get along with other dogs may well be a form of abuse and neglect. Most of the private training that owners seek involves dogs that are aggressive with other dogs. When a dog has the opportunity of interplay with other dogs, he learns how to be friendly and confident with both other dogs and people. Without the right kind of social experience, however, behaviour problems develop.

Pay Attention to Play Styles

Rowdy puppies should not be allowed to play roughly for long periods of time. By getting these types of dogs to play with other dogs of varying personality types – ranging from shy puppies to outgoing puppies, adolescent and adult dogs (who are not as tolerant of rude puppy antics) – you have the best chance of teaching the boisterous puppy how to adjust his play style to any dog, shy or not.

Letting a rowdy puppy play only with other rowdy puppies is asking for trouble. This pup will grow up to be obnoxious around other dogs, and will not be well-liked. Obnoxious adult dogs are not tolerated well by other adult dogs because they have no manners. They jump, rough-and-tumble and mouth too roughly, and as a result they are often overcorrected by other dogs. The rowdy adult dog is often the dog that all the other dogs pile upon because they feel he needs to be taught a lesson. The rowdy puppy needs lots of social experience: consider a day kennel to help him meet all kinds of dogs that will teach him the rules of socializing and getting along with the group.

To preserve your dog's healthy social development, monitor his playmates so that he's not playing too roughly for too long a period of time. Some rough play is acceptable, but too much will teach your puppy that being out of control is the way to play. Vary your dog's experience by going to new places and meeting lots of different dogs.

Playful puppies are the middle-of-the-road types; they can play roughly with the rowdy dog or tone it down to play with the shyer dogs. They are born peacemakers and party dogs. These puppies can be with any type of dog and have a great experience. At our day kennel we call this type of dog a 'cheerleader'. This is the dog that will invite any dog to play and be the most easygoing dog in the group.

Owners of this type of puppy need to be careful that their puppies don't get too overwhelmed by more enthusiastic dogs. Don't be afraid to initiate little breaks in the action, and let your dog calm down a bit before sending him back in for more fun.

Wallflowers

Unlike rowdy or energetic puppies, shy dogs have a tendency to wilt in a group of rowdy puppies, learning to be nervous and defensive, or sometimes aggressive, instead of playful. These dogs should spend huge amounts of time with playful puppies that invite them to play but are not too boisterous. Playful puppies invite shy dogs to interact by play bowing, barking (not excessively) and kissing the other puppy. The playful puppy will continue to invite the shy puppy to play until eventually he wears any resistance down.

A shy puppy needs triple the amount of social experience as the average dog, but it needs to be carefully calculated so as not to overwhelm him. If you own a shy puppy, enroll it in a well-organized puppy obedience class, as well as considering a carefully selected day kennel. Make sure that the kennels know how to socialize a shy dog and provide quiet periods via a nap in a crate or separate room several times a day.

Labrador Cross targets a hand with his nose

Socialization With People

The easiest part of socializing a puppy simply involves showing up in public with a clicker and treats to make sure that all new experiences are fun and rewarding. Bring plenty of delicious treats and a toy to keep the puppy under control. Go to parks and pet shops, or visit friends and family. Take your puppy to as many new places as possible; let him hear, see and experience the world. Be careful how you introduce your puppy to these new experiences, however: if he seems afraid or unsure of himself, go slowly. Try backing off a bit, using your best treats and happy voice to encourage your puppy to investigate.

Never force an unwilling puppy to investigate something it's frightened of; a bad experience can set you back weeks. Building confidence is a slow process, which works best if you provide your puppy with proof that the world is a safe and interesting place.

When a puppy is nervous of new people and strange things, the best way to help build his confidence is to let him take his time warming up and reward his bravery. A dog can't learn anything when it is afraid – so don't force him. By working at your dog's comfort level, you are putting money in the bank for building confidence. Keep the experience fun, upbeat and varied, and your puppy will develop into a confident adult dog.

Start Early

The more early intervention you can provide, the easier it will be for your puppy to learn to cope with new experiences. By having some tricks up your sleeve, you will have more options in helping your puppy to have good experiences, regardless of the circumstances.

1. Teach your puppy how to target your hand (see Chapter 4), and use this to introduce new people and objects.
2. Work at your puppy's comfort level, with the target being to gradually get him closer.
3. Go to at least two new places each week.
4. Continue to help your dog have good experiences, despite the extra effort this may require.
5. Get out there – you can do damage by waiting.

6. Continue past 16–18 weeks of age, but start sooner if possible (once your puppy has had his second set of vaccinations).
7. Enlist the help of family and friends.
8. Break scary new experiences into small attainable goals.
9. Avoid moving too fast; if you overwhelm your puppy, don't be afraid to stop and try again later.

Some Dogs Need More Social Experience

Depending on your dog's breed and personality, he may need more social experience than the average dog. The working and herding breeds are notoriously more suspicious of new people and experiences. If you think about what these dogs do for work, it makes a lot of sense. Working and herding dogs are bred to notice what is different and react to it, which is what makes them so good at herding and guarding. No wonder they need double the amount of socialization than the average dog in order to differentiate between friend and foe. The more good experiences they have, the more able they will be to accept new people and things as a normal part of their world.

What About Day Kennels?

A day centre may be available in your area (check Yellow Pages or ask your vet), and provides dogs with non-stop canine fun. Active dogs enjoy wrestling and playing with other dogs, and they get lots of attention from the staff. Taking your dog to day kennels a few times a week or every day can make a huge difference in the hours you spend together at home and on the weekends. Most working people come home too tired to exercise an active dog for two hours. With day kennels, however, that same owner could spend those two hours enjoying her dog in some other way.

Day care is a great way to give an active dog an outlet for all his energy, a shy dog an opportunity for new experiences, and a boisterous dog a chance to meet all kinds of dogs so as to learn how to adjust his play style to the dogs he's playing with. Following are some tips for searching for the right day centre.

- The dogs should have their own water bowls to help prevent the spread of viruses.
- The dogs should be separated into groups according to age, personality and play style, with no more than 10–15 dogs per group.
- An enhanced rest time via crates, separate mats or runs should be part of the day. This ensures that active dogs learn self-control, and shy or playful ones get a break from the other dogs.
- There should be one attendant for every 10 dogs.
- Day care attendants should be adults who have been properly trained in normal (and abnormal) dog behaviour, including how to safely break up a dogfight.
- A strong disinfectant and anti-viral solution should be used to clean up accidents.
- All dogs should be required to be vaccinated and wormed, spayed or neutered.
- All dogs should be in good health and not have symptoms of vomiting or diarrhoea, eye discharge or a cough.
- Dogs that are aggressive towards people or other dogs should not be allowed at day kennels for the safety of everyone.
- Go in person to meet the staff and see how they run their day, and make sure the indoor and outdoor facilities are clean and secure.

The best candidates for day kennels are puppies and young adult dogs. If you are unable to get your dog out to lots of different places to play with other dogs, day kennels may be a good option for you.

Why have your dog vaccinated?
Having your puppy vaccinated at eight weeks of age gives him immunity against certain diseases. You need to get your puppy out and about with other dogs as early as possible, so talk to your vet about a vaccination regime that will achieve protection at a young age.

Most day kennels will interview you, which gives you the opportunity to see the facility and ask questions. They will want to see a current vaccination certificate before agreeing to kennel your dog. Go with a checklist and be sure you are comfortable with the kennels; visit several places and talk to other dog owners before you make your decision.

Abused or Unsocialized?

Many dog owners mistakenly assume that their adopted or rescued dog was abused because he is shy or aggressive around new people or dogs. Such dogs tend to cower and shake or act aggressively, lunging and barking. Often the reality is that the dog has not been socialized with people, dogs and new experiences, and reacts aggressively or shyly out of fear and lack of confidence.

The best way to help a dog that behaves in this manner is to train him and build his confidence around new people, dogs and experiences. Making excuses for shy or aggressive dogs or trying to cuddle and comfort them will not solve the problem, and could make it worse. Remedial socialization (socializing a dog after the optimum age of eight to 18 weeks) is time-consuming and fraught with regression and frustration, but is ultimately well worth the effort. Some socialization tips for shy or aggressive dogs include:

1. Teach your dog how to target your hand, and extend the action to people and objects.
2. Build confidence slowly by taking your time and allowing for regression at any time.
3. Increase the distance by backing away from the person or object until the dog is comfortable.
4. If you are working with new people, get them to be as neutral as possible. Ask them to turn to the side, make no direct eye contact with the dog, and let it be the dog's idea to go to them.
5. Use the best treats; you want to associate new experiences with the things the dog really likes. Ox liver baked hard in a microwave with a little garlic, then broken into small pieces, is a strong, tasty treat.

Choose Your Dog's Playmates Carefully

Don't wait until your dog is fully vaccinated to begin socializing him, but do carefully choose the dogs he meets and plays with. It isn't a good idea to take a pup that is between eight and 12 weeks old to the local park and let it meet just any old dog or eat other dogs' faeces. Enroll your young dog in a well-organized puppy training class before he is 16 weeks old, and make sure that all the puppies attending the class have been started on their vaccinations.

A varied social experience is an insurance policy against a dog's future behaviour. Because he will have a lot of experience to draw upon, he will be able to enjoy the experience of being with other dogs.

Most puppies get their last series of injections at 12–14 weeks, but if you wait until your dog is that old to get him mixing with other dogs, you will probably find that he is shy and defensive and not as outgoing and adventurous as he might have been at an earlier age. This is a sign that the socialization window is closing and you need to increase and intensify his experience around other dogs. In short, if you wait to begin your dog's socialization until he is fully vaccinated, you will find you have to work harder at getting him to like being around other dogs.

More dogs die every year from behaviour problems resulting from a lack of socialization than dogs exposed to the more common viruses that we vaccinate against. So get out there and make sure every puppy you ever own from now on gets to meet lots of other dogs and people so he avoids becoming another statistic.

CHAPTER 21

Canine Public Relations

Everywhere you look, there are restrictions on dogs. A 'No Dogs Allowed' policy has been adopted by parks, hotels and beaches across the country. Things are changing slowly, however, due to an enormous education effort aimed at teaching dog owners how to be more responsible for their dogs and considerate towards the non-dog-owning public.

Be a Goodwill Ambassador

Though you may consider your pet your child, it's important to remember that not everyone shares your enthusiasm. People who don't like dogs often have had experiences with inconsiderate and irresponsible dog owners, who allow their dogs to bark all day and night, or early in the morning, leave unscooped poop on lawns or pavements, let their dog run off the lead through other people's gardens, and generally allow their dogs to be out of control. Being a goodwill ambassador for dogs means taking care not to allow your dog to intrude on someone else's space unless invited. Showing responsibility by example is the greatest way to ensure that more people can take dogs to more places.

The law to keep your dog on a lead exists in most residential communities and is often enforced only when someone complains to the local council or police. Fines vary from town to town, but repeat offenses are not looked kindly upon. Be considerate of your fellow citizens and make sure your dog does not run loose in the neighbourhood.

Basic Dog-Walking Manners

Taking your dog for a walk through your neighbourhood or the local park can be a wonderfully relaxing way to enjoy a beautiful day, but you should observe some basic good dog owner's etiquette so that everyone can enjoy the great outdoors. Be a responsible dog owner:

· Walk your dog on a lead in your neighbourhood and don't allow him to urinate or mark people's property, which includes trees, bushes and posts, and so on.
· Take care to train your dog to obey Leave It with regard to leg-lifting, to cut short his effort to claim others' property as his own.
· When you allow your dog freedom off the lead, make sure he is reliable with Leave It and Come. A dog that lacks training in these areas does not belong off the lead.

- If your dog is aggressive towards people or dogs, he should never be allowed off his lead in public places.
- Before you release your dog from the lead, look around you and make sure he won't be disturbing other people who may be walking or picnicking in the park.
- Don't allow your dog to jump on people, even if he's friendly; put your foot on the lead to prevent jumping, and teach him to Sit.
- Always carry a few plastic bags with you and clean up after your dog.
- Supervise your dog closely around other dogs or children to make sure no one is getting overexcited.

 Besides annoying your neighbours, loose dogs often eat things they shouldn't, dig up other people's lawns and get hit by cars. Keeping your dog safely at home will mean he gets to live out his life in a fun, safe environment provided by someone who loves him and wants him to live to a ripe old age.

Whether you are walking in your neighbourhood, taking your dog to the local park or beach for a romp or striding out in the woods, paying attention to basic good-dog-owner etiquette will ensure that others who come after you will be able to enjoy their dogs in the same places. Dog owners who are careful to manage their dog's behaviour in public pass on a lasting image to the people around them that dogs deserve access to public places. If you are tired of public places banning dogs, this is one small way to change the image the public has of out-of-control dogs running amok and creating havoc.

Poop-Scooping

There is no excuse for not picking up after your dog. Carry plastic bags with you every time you are out with your dog, and scoop regardless of whether anyone is looking or not! No one, not even the most ardent dog lover, likes stepping in canine faeces. There are lots of new products on the market today that make the scooping job easy. You can use any type of plastic bag, but the kind that reclose or tie are cheap and easy, and have the added benefit of sealing in the smell. Just turn the bag inside out, scoop the pile, carefully turn the bag the right side out, and zip or tie it.

There are many different poop bag holders available. Some can be attached to the lead and not only carry spare bags, but have places for your keys and change as well. Cleaning up after your dog announces to all around you that you are a responsible dog owner and that you care about how your pet affects others.

Nuisance Barkers

If your dog is a barker, don't leave it outside to practise its barking. If there is one thing that sends people over the edge, it's an incessantly barking dog. Dogs are pack animals that want to be with their families; they don't like to be left out, and will express frustration and boredom through persistent barking. If you have a barking problem with your dog, you owe it to yourself, your dog and your neighbours to address it and train your dog not to bark. Be considerate towards your neighbours: don't leave your dog outside in the early morning or late at night if you know he will bark at the slightest noise. Nothing makes neighbours more angry than a dog that wakes them up early in the morning or keeps them from getting to sleep at night.

Review the many ways to train your dog to stop barking (see Chapter 12), and become familiar with the reasons and causes why most dogs bark and how best to teach them not to. Here are some tips for curbing barking behaviour:

· **Provide plenty of exercise.** One to two hours a day of running, swimming, playing with other dogs and so on is essential. Consider a day kennel or care centre in your area.
· **Block the view.** Use shrubs, a fence or some other barrier so your dog cannot see who's passing by.
· **Provide mental stimulation.** Stuff Kong toys with peanut butter and dog food, and let your dog get all his meals out of his toys.

· **Meet your dog's needs.** Spend time with your dog and learn how to communicate with him. Enroll in a training class that uses fun, positive methods, such as the clicker training in this book, that teach your dog how to think.

· **Avoid the 'quick fix'.** Resist the temptation to buy devices that claim to stop your dog from barking. They either don't work or use too harsh a correction; train your dog instead.

Leaving a Dog in a Car

In addition to being responsible *for* their dogs, dog owners are also responsible *to* their dogs. Responsible dog owners do not leave their dogs in cars on days when the temperature is over 21°C (70 °F), even with the windows down. Dogs can quickly succumb to heatstroke and die if left for as little as 10 minutes in an enclosed car on a warm day. Even with the air conditioning on, things can happen, such your car stalling or running out of petrol. If you go out on a warm day, don't take a chance with your best friend's life: leave your dog at home where he is safe and comfortable.

The sun beating down on your car on a cool day can dramatically change the temperature in the car and make it uncomfortably hot. If you take your dog with you in the car, check on him frequently and make sure that he isn't becoming too hot or uncomfortable.

If the temperature is not too hot or too cold and you do decide to take your dog with you, make sure that he has adequate ventilation, but don't put the windows down so far that he could jump out and get lost or hit by a passing car. Be sure to remove his lead and training collar, if he's wearing one, so that it doesn't get caught on anything and strangle him. Make sure that if you do leave your dog in the car it's not in full sun, even if the day is cool.

Reliable Recall and Other Owner Issues

In general, your dog should only be off the lead if he Comes 100 per cent of the time, has a good strong Leave It command and does not jump on people he meets. With those three commands in place, you can reasonably control an off-lead dog. If you find that your dog is less than ideal in these areas, provide more training and practice before letting him loose on the public. Remember that everyone who meets your dog should come away with the feeling that your dog is a sweet and gentle creature that enhances the life of its owners. If you're vigilant about your dog's manners, even non-dog-people will come to appreciate the value of proper dog ownership.

These are the basics of good off-lead manners:

· Teach reliable Come, Leave It and Off commands.
· Teach your dog to Sit instead of jumping.
· Teach your dog to Sit for thrown objects such as balls and toys, and discourage jumping or mouthing for toys.
· Use a lead around groups of people, especially small children or people who are eating.
· Don't allow your dog to lift his leg on people's property, especially doorways, car tyres, bushes, lawn statues and so on.
· Teach your dog to wait for permission to say hello to other dogs; not all dogs are friendly, and they may not want to say hello.

Even if your dog is extremely friendly with other dogs and you trust him off the lead, be considerate of dogs that are on a lead and don't allow your dog to greet another dog without the owner's permission. Many dogs are aggressive with other dogs, and responsible owners of this type of dog manage their dogs' behaviour by keeping them on a lead at all times. Respect other dogs' and owners' space, and call your dog away.

Aggression

Aggression among dogs is mainly due to the fact that they lacked early socialization. If your dog does not like other dogs, do not allow him off the lead where there are other dogs. Avoid taking your dog to places where he is certain to be defensive and afraid, thus making you both miserable. If your dog is aggressive towards people, walk and exercise him at a time of day when no one else is around, in order to avoid confrontations. Be vigilant about not allowing people to interact with your dog if he has any history of biting people. Enlist the help of a qualified professional dog trainer to help you with these problems, and don't take chances.

Public Education

The more education exists about responsible dog ownership, the more receptive the public will be towards dogs. Consider forming an association of responsible dog owners in your area.

Getting dog-owning neighbours, relatives and friends to comply with pooper-scooper laws, lead training and overall pet-owner responsibility makes a giant step towards the acceptance of dogs in public spaces.

Cleaning up after your dog and respecting other people's property and space are ways that you can help educate the public about responsible dog ownership. Encouraging other dog owners to do the same is crucial to ensuring that dog lovers everywhere get to enjoy their dogs in public places.

The Best Canine Public Relations Option

Therapy dogs visit people in hospitals and nursing homes nationwide and make enormous differences in people's lives. Therapy dogs should be trained in obedience and in general have a sweet personality and love to be with people. There are several different organizations that certify dogs for this type of work.

Becoming a member of a therapy-dog organization will not only help provide you with insurance coverage, but, more importantly, it will give you the benefit of belonging to an organization that supports and guides the use of animals in hospitals and nursing homes.

Two Welsh Terriers and an Airedale Terrier

The work of a therapy dog is varied. It may simply be a visit involving cuddling or petting, or something more complicated, such as a speech lesson or physical therapy session. Regardless of its intensity, a visit from a therapy dog can change the course of a patient's treatment. There are countless stories of people talking for the first time or reaching some elusive milestone because of the presence of a dog.

Dogs can lighten the mood and make the work of rehabilitation in therapy a little less gruelling. In nursing homes across the country, dogs take long, lonely, endless days and make them something to look forward to. Dogs can truly make a difference in a patient's life and give them hope. Therapy dogs have been helping people cope with life for decades. A therapy dog is a dog whose pure intelligence, beauty and love are put to the best use possible.

Improve Your Dog's Image

Large, dark-coloured dogs often make some people a little nervous. Why not teach a scary-looking dog a silly trick to lighten people up. When a stranger who is afraid of your German Shepherd or Pit Bull sees your dog playing dead, who has time to be afraid? Can you picture a big black Great Dane saying its prayers or waving hello? Non-dog-lovers have often had a bad experience with a dog that has left them suspicious of dogs that look tough or are dark in colour (maybe it's because they can't see their facial expressions). Help change their experience not only by making sure that your dog is well-mannered, but also by teaching your dog a silly trick to perform that will make it a fun and memorable encounter.

No matter how friendly you know your dog to be, keep in mind that not everyone feels the same way about dogs as you do. Respect people's concern, and keep your distance until they invite your dog to greet them. Children especially may be worried, and should never be forced to greet or make contact with a dog.

Dogs bring a lot of joy to those around them when they are trained and cared for by the people who love them. By educating yourself and your dog, you are investing in your enjoyment of your dog and the interactions he has with those around him. Spread the word, set the example and show the world that owning a dog is an experience that no one should miss.

APPENDIX A

Resources

Useful Addresses

The Kennel Club
1–5 Clarges Street
London W1Y 8AB
Tel: 0870 606 6750
www.the-kennel-club.org.uk
info@the-kennel-club.org.uk

The Irish Kennel Club
Unit 36, Greenmount Office Park
Harolds Cross Bridge, Dublin 6W
Republic of Ireland
www.ikc.ie

National Dog Tattoo Register
PO Box 572, Harwich CO12 3SY
Tel: 01255 552455
www.dog-register.co.uk
info@dog-register.co.uk

Pro-Dogs and Pets as Therapy
Rocky Bank, 4 New Road,
Ditton, Kent ME20 6AD
Tel: 01732 848499
www.prodog.org.uk

British Veterinary Association
7 Mansfield Street
London W6 9NQ
Tel: 020 7636 6541
www.bva.co.uk

Dogs' Homes and Charities

Dogs Home, Battersea, London
Tel: 020 7622 3626

Dogs' Home, Birmingham
Tel: 0121 643 5211

Dogs' Home, Wood Green, Essex
Tel: 0176 383 8329

Dogs' Home, Lothian, Scotland
Tel: 0131 660 5842

Blue Cross
Tel: 0171 835 4224

National Boarding Kennel Federation
Tel: 020 8995 8331

Dogs' Trust
Tel: 020 7837 0006

PDSA
Tel: 01952 290999

RSPCA
Tel: 08705 555999

Magazines and Newspapers

Dog World (weekly newspaper)
Somerfield House, Wottan Road,
Ashford, Kent TN23 6LW
Tel: 01233 621877
www.dogworld.co.uk
editorial@dogworld.co.uk

Dogs Today *(magazine)*
Town Mill, Bagshot Road
Chobham, Surrey GU24 8BZ
Tel: 01276 858860
dogstoday@dial.pipex.com

APPENDIX B

Bibliography

There are literally thousands of books and pamphlets on the subject of dogs and training, and the standard varies between each one. The selection below is one I have found useful, but it is in no way intended to be definitive.

If your local bookshop does not stock the titles below, check their availability on *Amazon.co.uk*.

Abrantes, Roger, *Dog Language: An Encyclopedia of Canine Behaviour*

Benjamin, Carol, *Dog Problems*

Brunner, David, and Stall, Sam, *The Dog Owner's Manual: Operating Instructions, Trouble-shooting Tips and Advice on Lifetime Maintenance*

Campbell, William E, *Owner's Guide to Better Behaviour in Dogs*

Campbell, William E, *Behaviour Problems in Dogs*

Cantrell, Krista, *Catch Your Dog Doing Something Right: How to Train Any Dog in Five Minutes a Day*

Coren, Stanley, *How to Speak Dog: Mastering the Art of Dog–Human Communication*

Donaldson, Jean, *The Culture Clash*

Donaldson, Jean, *Dogs Are from Neptune*

Drakeford, J, *Holistic Dog*

Dunbar, Dr Ian, *Dog Behaviour*

Dunbar, Dr Ian, *How to Teach a New Dog Old Tricks*

Evans, Job Michael, *Training and Explaining: How to Be the Dog Trainer You Want to Be*

Fennell, Jan, *The Dog Listener: Learn How to Communicate with Your Dog*

Fisher, Betty, and Delzio, Suzanne, *So Your Dog's Not Lassie*

Fisher, John, *Dogwise: The Natural Way to Train Your Dog*

Fox, Dr Michael W, *Understanding Your Dog*

Giffin, James M, *Dog Owner's Home Veterinary Handbook*

Hodgson, S, *Dog Tricks for Dummies*

Kearey, Ian (ed.), *Looking After Your Dog*

Larkin, Peter, and Stockman, Mike, *The Ultimate Encyclopedia of Dogs, Dog Breeds and Dog Care*

Milani, Myrna, DVM, *The Body Language and Emotions of Dogs*

Milani, Myrna, DVM, *DogSmart*

Owens, Paul, *The Dog Whisperer: A Compassionate, Nonviolent Approach to Dog Training*

Pryor, Karen, *Karen Pryor on Behaviour: Essays and Research*

Pryor, Karen, *Don't Shoot the Dog: The New Art of Teaching and Training*

Reid, Pamela, PhD, *Excel-Erated Learning: Explaining in Plain English How Dogs Learn and How Best to Teach Them*

Rugaas, Turid, *On Talking Terms with Dogs: Calming Signals*

Ryan, Terry, *The Toolbox for Remodelling Your Problem Dog*

Schwartz, Charlotte, *The Howell Book of Puppy Raising*

Scott, John Paul, and Fuller, John L, *Genetics and the Social Behaviour of the Dog*

Volhard, Jack, and Volhard, Wendy, *Dog Training for Dummies*

Wilkes, Gary, *A Behaviour Sampler*

Index